CHRISTLike
Discipleship

JUAN VASQUEZ

Cover design by Juan J. Vasquez

Cover picture, "Jesus standing with his feet in the sand on a beach," by Forgiven Photography from Lightstock.com

ISBN-13: 978-0-9991254-4-1

ISBN E-book: 978-0-9991254-5-8

Printed in the U.S.A.

ENDORSEMENTS

Pastor Vasquez does a wonderful job in making the reader conscious of being intentional with living and provoking others towards a Christlike lifestyle of true biblical discipleship.

- Dr. Juan A. Garcia
Administrative Bishop of the Hispanic
Northeast Region of the Church of God

If you want to know what it means to be a disciple of Christ you should read this book by Pastor Juan Vasquez, *Christlike: Discipleship*. It is well written. Clear. Understandable. With a gift for communicating and teaching, that not every writer possesses, Pastor Juan shows us the identity, characteristics, and mission of a follower of Christ. I highly recommend that you read this book because it will inspire you, challenge you, and change your life.

- Dr. Guillermo Flores,
National Latino Coach and pastor of the
Miami Melrose Free Methodist Church USA.
Professor of Asbury Theological Seminary.

"We need to become Christlike," says Pastor Juan... This book pulls no punches. From the moment you dive into it until the moment you reach the shore on the other side of this ocean of exhortation, you will find yourself repeatedly confronted with a question that even serves as the title of one of the chapters: "What Kind of Disciple Do You Want to Be?"

- Evangelist David Martinez

TABLE OF CONTENTS

FOREWORD

"You're from New York?! But where is your accent?!" So goes one of the most frequent questions I hear from people as I travel the States. I find such a question to be both funny and intriguing: funny because I have unintentionally shocked someone, intriguing because I wonder what exactly the individual has in mind when he or she thinks of a New York accent. Inevitably, I end up wondering to myself, "What is a New York accent anyway?" If I'm feeling extra sociological that day, I wonder about the origin of accents and what factors contribute to the development of the intonations that permeate any given local culture.

Yet another different and more humorous matter is where people get their ideas of what certain accents should sound like. Sometimes I disappoint my listener and sometimes I don't (like when I inform them that "I don't drink *Kaw-fee*[1]"). After all, it's not unreasonable to expect people to generally sound like where they're from. I guess I am a New Yorker after all.

In many ways the modern church has lost its accent. We have left the world flabbergasted as they ask with a confused look, "Oh, are you a Christian? I couldn't tell." It seems that what has happened to us is the same thing that many others have experienced when they relocate to another state or country. At first, the individual experiences what many call "culture shock," the psychological impact of being in a strange land or a foreign culture. But eventually, we get over it. Assimilation works its magic and before long we fit in, sometimes so well that our own

---

[1] Or, as the rest of the English-speaking world says: "Coffee."

culture is swallowed whole by other priorities. Our traditions quietly disappear, our idiosyncrasies fade, our tastes morph, our differences are flattened out, and we become just like everyone else. This may not be too serious if we are talking about trading a savory "mangu" for a spicy burrito. But it certainly becomes a problem if we are talking about followers of Christ no longer wanting to be like Him.

"We need to become Christlike," says Pastor Juan, "and if the will of God was Jesus' focus and North Star, shouldn't it be ours?" Such words may summarize the author's heart and intention throughout this literary work. This book pulls no punches. From the moment you dive into it until the moment you reach the shore on the other side of this ocean of exhortation, you will find yourself repeatedly confronted with a question that even serves as the title of one of the chapters: "What Kind of Disciple Do You Want to Be?" Oh that more Christians took the time to reflect about the eternal matters that make the temporal matter.

I myself, being an itinerant preacher and teacher have had the privilege of meeting many people around the world, and have witnessed a very interesting phenomena: many of the very same people who crowd church buildings from Sunday to Sunday have little to no sense of purpose or meaning in their Christian life. As my late grandmother Luz Maria Martinez used to tell me, "the churches are full but the people are empty!" Tragically, not much has changed since she entered her eternal rest at the end of 2017. Unfortunately, this has created a problem that goes far beyond a mere revolving door,[2] it actually bars people's entrance into the Kingdom of God. This is manifested in the utter lack of commitment the modern church has toward reaching the lost.

By building his arguments on the firm foundation of God's Word, Pastor Vasquez reminds his reader that the great commission is not just one option among many. "It is not for full-time pastors, evangelists, teachers, or ministers. Every follower of Jesus must establish His kingdom here on earth!" Not too long after this exhortation, he puts his finger on the aching sore which afflicts the body of Christ: "For too long we have relegated making disciples to the pastor or leaders of the church." Reading this book, I often gave a reluctant "amen." Reluctant, not because the truth therein was ambiguous, questionable, or not nuanced enough. But rather, the problems described in the work were painful to admit.

As stated previously, having grown up in New York City comes with its entertaining perks, one of which is the ability to enjoy the different colors, accents, and cultures that saturate the boroughs: from the Dominicans and Puerto Ricans in the Bronx, to the African American brothers in Harlem, to the Italians downtown, or the West Indians in Queens, every culture has its beautiful distinctives. But what would happen if they all decided to eradicate what makes them each different? What would ensue is a bland world in which everyone is a mere clone of one another. While a true disciple of Christ has indeed been called to mimic his Lord, as will be argued throughout this book,

---

[2] A phrase often used to describe a sociological situation in which people get involved in the church and later lose interest, thus resulting in an "in-and-out" kind of approach to service unto one another.

what seems to have happened to the church is not simply *inactivity* or *passivity*, but bold and brazen disobedience.

If repentance is sometimes defined as "making an about face" or a "change of mind/heart," this interesting type of disobedience of the Body today is strange indeed. A parable might highlight the point:

A certain son had been forgiven by his merciful father after having squandered his inheritance on wasteful living. At first, the memory of how his father celebrated him when he returned home was ever fresh on his mind. In fact, he had a picture of it framed on his bedroom wall. However, as months turned into years, the gratitude began to fade and the effects of familiarity began to invade his soul. Soon after, he began to ask his father for money again and again. The asking wasn't really a problem; it was how he asked that bothered the father. "Is this all you can give me now?!" the son would often snicker. "Son," the father would respond with great sadness, "don't you remember how you wasted all of your inheritance and even so I took you back into the house and restored you? How could you be so lazy now?"

The son never really understood the father's complaining, and would never really mention his dad to his friends. In fact, his friends sometimes were curious about how he still had a place to live. "After all," they thought, "didn't he spend his whole inheritance? How did he end up still with a roof over his head?" Somehow, it never occurred to the son to tell anyone about what an awesome dad he had. Instead, he was too self-centered and complacent to even care.

Over the years, the son's ingratitude was becoming

too costly to the family's good name. His utter laziness and selective amnesia toward his father's goodness began to affect the household to the point that it kept others away. Eventually, the father had to ask his son to leave the house.

Sound familiar? It's just Luke 15 inverted.

May this book be the wind that shouts the Spirit of the living God back into this valley of dry bones that the church has become. May we embrace our true identity as followers of Christ – accent and all. You are in for both a treat and a challenge. Sit back and read prayerfully, perhaps with a cup of coffee in your hand. As we say in New York: "enjoy your KAW-fee!" Consider the book in your hands a call for Christians to recover more than our accents.

- Evangelist David Martinez

PREFACE

In our days, it's easy to look at Christian television or YouTube videos and see hundreds, thousands, or even millions of people coming to Christ for salvation. This of course is amazing and I rejoice to see these lives coming out of the kingdom of darkness and into the kingdom of light. Yet, I have noticed a problem with many churches. We are good at making converts but not good at making disciples. We are good at leading people to Christ but not so good at teaching them to follow Him.

In this book, I desire to speak about what it means to be a Christian, a disciple of Jesus Christ, and how to disciple others. This book is not an extensive and complete guide on this topic but just my thoughts on what I believe is essential to know.

For the purpose of providing a more comprehensive book on discipleship, I will be integrating a previous book I authored entitled, *Christlike: Following in His Footsteps*. You might consider this book a revised and expanded edition of that one. This book will be fresh and challenging to those who consider themselves Christians but it's also a great tool for new converts to get grounded as they begin their relationship with Christ. So feel free and encouraged to get a copy for any friends or family members that are seeking to mature in their walk with God.

I pray that you will not be the same after you read this book. My life was certainly impacted by the ideas presented here. May God grant us grace to continue to grow in our commitment to the Lord Jesus Christ.

FOUNDATIONS:
THE CALL AND COST OF FOLLOWING JESUS

Introduction
TRUE DISCIPLESHIP

God's plan from the beginning was to make a people that looked like Him. Genesis 1:26-27 says, "²⁶ Then God said, 'Let Us make man in Our image, according to Our likeness...' ²⁷ God created man in His own image, in the image of God He created him; male and female He created them." But when man disobeyed God, that image became tainted with sin. And so every man that was born after Adam was brought to the earth with Adam's sinful nature, which was now corrupt and dead.

Even so, God's plan did not change. He sent His son, Jesus, into this world, and He became the visible image of the invisible God (Colossians 1:15). Hebrews 1:3 says that Christ "is the radiance of His glory and the exact representation of His nature." He was conceived by the Holy Spirit, was born of the virgin Mary and through this miraculous birth God became a man through Jesus and lived among us (John 1:1, 14).

As a man, Jesus showed us what God's intention for mankind was. He lived a perfect, holy, righteous, sinless life; a life of love, full of power and in complete fellowship with God. He modeled for us what was God's will for our lives. He became like us so that we might become like Him (2 Corinthians 5:21).

And so when God calls us to salvation, He is calling us back to His original purpose - to look like Him. His desire is to do so by conforming our lives to Jesus. "For those whom He foreknew, He also predestined *to become* conformed to the image of His Son" (Romans

8:29). This is true discipleship: the process or journey of being conformed to the image of Christ, who is the exact image of God.

This is the reason why Jesus would not normally say, "receive me" or "accept me" or "let me come into your heart"[3] when calling people to become His disciples. Frequently, Jesus' invitation to those who would become His disciples was "follow me."

To Matthew He said, "Follow me!" (Matthew 9:9). To Peter, Andrew, James, and John He said, "follow me and I will make you fishers of men" (Mark 1:17; Matthew 4:19). To the rich young ruler who was seeking eternal life He said, "sell all that you possess and distribute it to the poor, and you shall have treasure in heaven; and come, follow Me" (Luke 18:22). And He tells everyone who wants to be called a Christian, "deny yourself, pick up your cross and follow me" (Luke 9:23).

This is the true call of discipleship - to follow Jesus in order to become more like Him. So, are you following Him? I'm not asking if you go to church. I'm not asking if you pray, read your Bible, listen to Christian music, or speak in tongues. I'm asking you, "are you following Jesus?"

Scot McKnight says, "Those who aren't following Jesus aren't his followers. It's that simple. Followers follow, and those who don't follow aren't followers. To follow Jesus means to follow Jesus into a society where justice rules, where love shapes everything. To follow Jesus

---

[3] This does not mean that these expressions are not biblical or that we shouldn't use them when leading a person to salvation in Christ. See for example John 1:12 or Revelation 3:20.

4

means to take up his dream and work for it."[4]

God's desire is for you to follow Jesus and conform your life to His. Only then, will you truly be a Christian, a disciple, and a follower of Jesus. "God loves you just the way you are, but he refuses to leave you that way. More than anything, he wants you to be just like Jesus."[5]

---

[4] *One Life: Jesus Calls, We Follow* (Grand Rapids, MI: Zondervan, 2010), 70.
[5] Max Lucado, *Just Like Jesus* (Nashville, Tennessee: W Publishing Group, 2003), XII.

Chapter 1
WHAT DOES IT MEAN TO FOLLOW CHRIST?

Are you a Christian? Do you know what that word means? A CHRIST-ian is a disciple of Christ. A disciple of Christ is a learner, imitator, and follower of Jesus Christ. So if you are a CHRIST-ian that means you are someone who is following in the footsteps of Jesus. If you are not following Him, then you are not a real Christian. You might bear the name, you might have confessed Him as your Lord and Savior; you might even be a faithful church-goer. But by definition, for you to be considered a Christian you must be following in the footsteps of Jesus.

Now, what does it mean to follow Jesus? We can't see Him with our eyes or touch Him with our hands. So how can we follow someone who isn't visible to us?

That is what this book is about. In the chapters to come, I will speak more in depth about what it looks like to follow Jesus, but I want to begin with this general thought. We can summarize what it means to follow Jesus in three simple words: OBEY, IMITATE, and REFLECT.

1. OBEY His teachings

If we want to follow in the footsteps of Jesus, we must learn to obey His teachings. John 8:31 says, "So Jesus was saying to those Jews who had believed Him, 'If you continue in My word, *then* you are truly disciples of Mine.'" According to this verse, there were Jews who had heard His message and seen His miracles and through these had come to believe in Him. But notice what He says to them, "If you **continue in My word**, *then* you are truly disciples of Mine" (emphasis mine).

Disciples are not just those who know the words of Christ. Disciples are not just those who memorize the words of Christ. Disciples are not just those who confess, teach or proclaim the words of Christ. Disciples are those who **continue** in His word. Those who walk in it, practice it, and obey. And they do this, not once, or twice, or for a period of time. They **continue**, they remain, they endure in it permanently.

You can distinguish a real Christian from a false one by their *continuing* in the words of Christ. This does not mean that they are perfect or never fail, but that even when they fall they get back up and *continue* in His words. Jesus even tells us that we can measure a person's love for Him by this very same attribute. Jesus told His disciples,

> "[15] If you love Me, you will keep My commandments... [21] He who has My commandments and keeps them is the one who loves Me; and he who loves Me will be loved by My Father, and I will love him and will disclose Myself to him"... [23] Jesus answered and said to him, "If anyone loves Me, he will keep My word; and My Father will love him, and We will come to him and make Our abode with him. [24] He who does not love Me does not keep My words; and the word which you hear is not Mine, but the Father's who sent Me." (John 14:15, 21, 23-24)

In other words, Jesus is not only interested in how you worship or sing, or if you are enthusiastic and shout and cry at the mention of His name. Those things are good, but Jesus also measures our love by our obedience to His words.

So if you intend to follow Jesus, the first thing you must do is obey His teachings.[6]

2. IMITATE His lifestyle

Following Jesus is not just about doing what He says, but also about living as He lived. We must imitate His lifestyle. We can summarize the way He lived in three words – power, love, and holiness.

Jesus lived a life of power. When Peter described Jesus' life to a group of Gentiles (non-Jews) he said, *"You know of* Jesus of Nazareth, how God anointed Him with the Holy Spirit and with power, and *how* He went about doing good and healing all who were oppressed by the devil, for God was with Him" (Acts 10:38). From His baptism to His death and resurrection, God displayed His power through Jesus. He healed the sick, He raised the dead, He cast out demons, He performed miracles, signs and wonders. God has made this same power available to us and expects us to follow in the footsteps of Jesus.

Jesus lived a life of love. Everything Jesus did was motivated by love. The Bible says that Jesus taught and fed the multitudes because He was moved by compassion (Matthew 9:36). The Bible says Jesus called sinners to Himself because He loved them (Mark 10:21). The Bible tells us Jesus even healed the sick, out of love and compassion (Mark 1:41). If we are going to imitate His life,

---

[6] For a general summary of His teachings read the Sermon on the Mount in Matthew 5-7.

we must love as He loves. Miracles, signs and wonders, and spiritual gifts mean nothing if there is no love (1 Corinthians 13:1-3).

Lastly, *Jesus lived a life of holiness*. Although He was tempted in every way, just like we are, the Bible says that He never sinned (Hebrews 4:15). He never gave into temptation. Through the word of God, He was able to resist and overcome Satan's temptations in the wilderness (Matthew 4:1-11). He overcame Satan's temptation, that came through the lips of one of His very own disciples, Peter, when he tried to dissuade Him from going to the cross (Matthew 16:23). He even overcame His own human will in the Garden of Gethsemane, when it seemed that the Father's cup would be too much to drink (Matthew 26:36-46).

It is because of Christ's victory over these temptations that God was able to present Jesus as a perfect, sinless sacrifice to redeem us and "take away the sins of the world" (John 1:29). And just like Jesus, we too must avoid sin and pursue holiness, "without which no one will see the Lord" (Hebrews 12:14).

3. REFLECT His heart

Up until now, all the other steps have mostly dealt with the exterior. But this last step also deals with the interior of every Christian. Not only must we obey His teachings and reflect His lifestyle, we must reflect His heart. We must pray and seek to desire what He desires, think what He thinks, hate what He hates, and love what He loves.

Jesus described His heart with the adjectives "gentle and humble" (Matthew 11:29). He was not a rude or proud man. He was not a tyrant or dictator who demanded respect and obedience. Rather, Jesus was the sort of person who was willing to serve those who were beneath Him, even if it meant He did the work of a slave (see John 13). Jesus said, "the Son of Man did not come to be served, but to serve, and to give His life a ransom for many" (Mark 10:45).

Paul recognized this quality in Jesus and summarized this last step for us in a beautiful creed sung by the early church,

> [5] Have this attitude in yourselves which was also in Christ Jesus, [6] who, although He existed in the form of God, did not regard equality with God a thing to be grasped, [7] but emptied Himself, taking the form of a bond-servant, *and* being made in the likeness of men. [8] Being found in appearance as a man, He humbled Himself by becoming obedient to the point of death, even death on a cross. [9] For this reason also, God highly exalted Him, and bestowed on Him the name which is above every name, [10] so that at the name of Jesus every knee will bow, of those who are in heaven and on earth and under the earth, [11] and that every tongue will confess that Jesus Christ is Lord, to the glory of God the Father. (Philippians 2:5-11)

It is because of this that we too should be willing to be humble ourselves and treat others gently, and be willing to serve them no matter our title, position, or status.

Putting it all together

The true call of discipleship is a call to conform ourselves to the image of God. This is best done by following Jesus. And what does it mean to follow Jesus? It means (1) We should OBEY His teachings; (2) We should IMITATE His life; and (3) We should REFLECT His heart and character.

Although we will focus on these things in more detail in the following chapters, I would like to bring up two very important themes in relation to following Jesus. The first has to do with the price we must consider to become a disciple. The second is a choice we must make once we are willing to pay that price.

Chapter 2
THE COST OF BEING A DISCIPLE

Have you ever gone shopping for clothes? If so, I imagine you are like me, at least in one way. Before I walk to the register with any clothes to pay I make sure to look at the price tag on the item. I do not want to go through the embarrassment of stepping up to the cash register, opening my wallet and right then and there, discovering that I do not have enough money to purchase the clothes I have chosen.

The clothes may be nice. They may be attractive. I may even imagine myself wearing them. But if I do not have enough money to actually make the purchase, I will not be walking out of that store with them. I would have to go back when I have enough.

The same principle applies to following Jesus, to being His disciple. There is a cost, a "price tag" on the "T-shirt" of discipleship. And unless you are willing or able to pay that amount you should not be walking out of the "store" with it on. The Bible has more to say about this in Luke chapter 14.

Luke begins by telling us the background for what is taking place in this chapter. The Bible first focuses on the audience that is around Jesus. It says, "Now large crowds were going along with Him…" (v25a).

Now, this large crowd followed Christ around for many reasons. They followed Him for the miracles, signs and wonders He was performing. They followed Him because of the fish and bread that He multiplied. Some just followed Him out of emotion or curiosity.

In the same way many people come to "church" or serve God for various reasons. Some come to "church" looking for boyfriends or girlfriends, some out of an emotional need, some are forced to come, some come because of tradition or custom, and some come because they have nothing better to do – they are bored.

So, Jesus turns to these people and tells them something; something hard, something important, something confrontational. He tells them that if they truly want to follow Him and be His disciples there is a price they must be willing to pay, there is a cost they have to consider. And what exactly are those costs?

Cost #1: to be a disciple of Christ we must love Him more than we love anyone else.

"25 Now large crowds were going along with Him; and He turned and said to them, 26 'If anyone comes to Me, and does not hate his own father and mother and wife and children and brothers and sisters, yes, and even his own life, he cannot be My disciple.'" (vv25-26)

At first glance, this verse may shock you. Is Christ actually telling us to "hate" our families and even ourselves? Aren't we supposed to honor our parents and love one another?

Don't worry, Christ is not calling us to "hate" in the sense of being hostile, angry, or against others. This word can also be translated "to love less."[7] In other words, yes, we should honor others and love others, but that honor and love for others, including ourselves, should be less than the honor and love we owe Christ. We must prefer Christ over

---

[7] Strong's #3404

anyone or anything. Christ must have first place in our lives. Our loyalty is to Him first. He must come before our father, mother, spouse, children, brother, sister and even our self.

This cost is so important. There are many people that live in nations or come from families where there are strong religious and traditional customs. Anyone who deviates or abandons these customs or traditions are automatically seen as traitors or apostates. As a result, many cultures, religious groups and even family members will reject, isolate, humiliate, persecute, or kill anyone who turns to Jesus. Maybe you are from one of those families or cultures.

But if we are going to follow Jesus, we must be willing to risk our lives for the sake of Christ. We must be willing to love Him and honor Him more than we would anyone else. We must be willing to risk being rejected, ostracized, or persecuted for His name sake. A person who loves their family or even their own life more than Jesus cannot be a disciple of Jesus.

Now why would Christ say this? Why should we love Jesus more than all these others? What makes Him worthy of this type of love or honor?

Although I could list many reasons for why we should love Him or what makes Him worthy of honor, I will just mention two. The first is that He is God! Jesus is God the Son, the second member of the Holy Trinity. He is the first and the last, the Alpha and the Omega, the beginning and the end, the author and the perfecter of our faith. He is the source of all life (John 1:3).

He is the one true God and there are no other gods besides Him. Before Him nor after Him were there any gods formed (Isaiah 43:10). As the Sovereign King of the universe, and as our creator, He commands us, in Exodus 20:3-4, "³ You shall have no other gods before me. ⁴ You shall not make for yourself an idol" in the form of anything. In other words, anything you put before God becomes your God or your idol. We are to worship God alone.

The second reason is, Jesus is the source of our salvation. Although Jesus is God, He put aside all the benefits of His divinity (Philippians 2:7). He humbled Himself and became a man in order to serve us (Philippians 7-8; Mark 10:45). Then God placed all of our sins, diseases and pains on Jesus and He died as a substitute for us on the cross. And through His punishment and stripes, we received healing and peace with God (Isaiah 53:4-6). Yet He did not stay dead. God raised Him up on the third day and made Him the source of our salvation. The Bible says, "There is salvation in no one else; for there is no other name under heaven that has been given among men by which we must be saved" (Acts 4:12).

If you turn away from Jesus where else will you find eternal life? (John 6:68). He gave it all to save you. Are you not willing to give it all to follow Him?

These are just two reasons why we should love Christ more than anyone or anything. These are just two reasons why He is worthy of our love and our loyalty.

Cost #2: to be a disciple of Christ we must be willing to carry our Cross.

"Whoever does not carry his own cross and come after Me cannot be My disciple." (v27)

Jesus very clearly states the second requirement or

cost someone must be willing to pay if they would like to be His disciple, His follower, and thus be called a genuine Christian. The person must be willing to carry their own cross and then follow Him.

The cross was an instrument of death. It was an ancient equivalent of the electric chair. Only it was far worse. It was a humiliating form of execution that Romans would use on slaves or non-Roman citizens to kill them slowly, by asphyxiation, while nailed to wood completely naked. In the mind of the people living in the time of Jesus, the cross only meant one thing – DEATH. Leonard Ravenhill has said, "Anyone who was seen carrying a cross knew already that they were a dead man walking."

But what does it mean for us to carry a cross? Should someone nail us to one physically? Or should we go into a forest or a Home Depot to get some wood, put it together, and walk around with it on our shoulders?

No. What Jesus is saying is that if you want to be His disciple, He is calling you to die to yourself, to deny yourself, to give up everything in order to follow Him.

You might have certain desires, attitudes, dreams, goals, plans, relationships, opinions and ideas but God is saying we must be willing to put all that to the side in order to obey Him and follow Christ. There is no halfway commitment. You give it all to God or you give Him nothing.

In the Gospels, there are these parables[8] that speak of this idea in a more illustrative way. Jesus said,

44 The kingdom of heaven is like a treasure

---

[8] A short story that teaches a lesson.

hidden in the field, which a man found and hid again; and from joy over it he goes and sells all that he has and buys that field. ⁴⁵ Again, the kingdom of heaven is like a merchant seeking fine pearls, ⁴⁶ and upon finding one pearl of great value, he went and sold all that he had and bought it. (Matthew 13:44-46)

So from these two stories we can see that the treasure and the pearl of great value represent the kingdom of God. The men in these stories represent you and me. In this world, once we come across God's kingdom, and we hear the message of the gospel, we must be willing to give up everything we own in order to receive it.

This is exactly what Paul, one of the main writers of the New Testament, did. Although he had great prestige, power, and position, he gave it all up in order to follow Jesus. These are his words,

⁷ But whatever things were gain to me, those things I have counted as loss for the sake of Christ. ⁸ More than that, I count all things to be loss in view of the surpassing value of knowing Christ Jesus my Lord, for whom I have suffered the loss of all things, and count them but rubbish so that I may gain Christ, ⁹ and may be found in Him... (Philippians 3:7-9a)

And in reference to his cross and following Jesus he said, "I have been crucified with Christ; and it is no longer I who live, but Christ lives in me; and the *life* which I now live in the flesh I live by faith in the Son of God, who loved me and gave Himself up for me" (Galatians 2:20).

The door to eternal life is narrow and whoever would want to enter it must walk the narrow path (Matthew 7:13-14). And that path is the path of the cross. That path is a path of death and self-denial.

Cost #3: to be a disciple of Christ we must be willing to love Him more than we love our material possessions

"So then, none of you can be My disciple who does not give up all his own possessions." (v33)

Jesus is not calling us here to sell everything we own and live a nomadic life on the streets, although it is possible for Him to call some to such a life (Luke 18:22). Nonetheless, His focus here is that whatever we own materially, physically, and financially would be given up to Him. So He would become the owner of what we have and we would become His stewards or asset managers.

Riches and money have a way of taking control of a person's heart and life (Matthew 13:22; 1 Timothy 6:9). Money isn't evil, but the love of money is (1 Timothy 6:10). Jesus even compared this love for money to a god called Mammon that governs many people's lives. He said, "No one can serve two masters; for either he will hate the one and love the other, or he will be devoted to one and despise the other. You cannot serve God and wealth [Mammon]" (Matthew 6:24; parenthesis mine).

It isn't wrong to be rich. But what God is looking for is our willingness to seek His kingdom first, and His righteousness, and then everything we need will be given to us (Matthew 6:33). And if at any moment Jesus should call upon us to give something up, we should be willing to do so. Whether it be our homes, money, careers or families, everything we have belongs to Him.

These are the costs for becoming a follower of Christ. But, why would Jesus say such hard things to these people? How could Jesus ask so much of them? I mean, doesn't Jesus want people to follow Him? Doesn't He want to expand His Kingdom, have many followers, and be popular? These sacrifices would cause many to turn away.

It did and it still does today.

He tells them this so that they don't start something that they won't be able to finish. (Remember the whole thing about going to the register without looking at the price tag?) Jesus uses two parables to illustrate this point.

The Parable of the Tower

"28 For which one of you, when he wants to build a tower, does not first sit down and calculate the cost to see if he has enough to complete it? 29 Otherwise, when he has laid a foundation and is not able to finish, all who observe it begin to ridicule him, 30 saying, 'This man began to build and was not able to finish.'" (vv28-30)

Can you see why Jesus has to tell them about the cost of following Him? It's because if they begin to follow Jesus but don't finish "building the tower," or running the race; if they don't persevere till the end, then the people around them will ridicule them, make fun of them, or even worse make fun of God. So instead of bringing glory to the name of Christ they will bring shame.

How many half built towers do we see around us? How many "Christians" have we seen start the path but not finish it?

I know someone who lived a very sinful and perverted life before giving his life to Jesus. His friends didn't believe he was sincere, and even if he was, that he wouldn't last too long. Their prediction came true. This person was enthusiastic, passionate and genuinely thankful of God for his salvation. But within a short period of time he had returned to his old sinful ways. The friends laughed and mocked, and their hearts were hardened towards the gospel. The reason? The backsliding of this man reinforced the idea that Christianity wasn't for them. It was too hard, so why even bother? If the gospel couldn't make a lasting difference in this man's life, how would it do so in theirs?

Maybe there are people around you waiting for you to backslide. Maybe those people don't believe in God and they don't believe in you. Perhaps they secretly want you to fail, so they can throw it in your face and reinforce whatever excuses they have for not serving God.

The Parable of a King Going to War

"31 Or what king, when he sets out to meet another king in battle, will not first sit down and consider whether he is strong enough with ten thousand men to encounter the one coming against him with twenty thousand? 32 Or else, while the other is still far away, he sends a delegation and asks for terms of peace." (vv31-32)

Jesus gives us another reason why we should count the cost, through this parable. He compares Christianity to a war. He explains to us that if we don't have the guts nor the means to fight to the end then we are going to die on the battlefield.

I want you to know that the call of salvation is not a call to a garden full of flowers and roses. It is a call to war.

21

Once you say "yes" to Jesus you have signed your life over to the army of the Lord. You must fight, you must train, you must endure. I've heard someone say, "The devil tries all he can to make sure a person never comes to Christ. But if they do, he will do all he can to keep them from being effective." By the end of his life, the apostle Paul said, "I have fought the good fight, I have finished the course, I have kept the faith" (2 Timothy 4:7).

Becoming a Christian means you will have all of hell against you but on the other side all of heaven will be with you. "Greater is He who is in you than he who is in the world" (1 John 4:4). "If God is for us, who can be against us?" (Romans 8:31 NIV).

How many soldiers of Christ have we seen die on the battlefield because they failed to understand this one point? Once we put our hands to the plow we cannot look back (Luke 9:62). I have seen many backsliders in worse condition after leaving Christ than when they first started following Him. The Bible says "For it would be better for them not to have known the way of righteousness, than having known it, to turn away from the holy commandment handed on to them" (2 Peter 2:21).

There are two reasons for this. First, the Bible says that the more knowledge you have the greater the judgment you will receive (Luke 12:47-48; James 3:1). In other words, if you choose to walk away from God, especially after knowing the truth, on the day of judgment there will not be any mercy for you (Hebrews 2:3; 10:29). Your judgment will be harder than someone who never knew Christ.

The second reason why we cannot turn back once

we've committed our lives to Jesus is that the Bible teaches us that our sinful condition can become 7 times worse.

> [24] When the unclean spirit goes out of a man, it passes through waterless places seeking rest, and not finding any, it says, "I will return to my house from which I came." [25] And when it comes, it finds it swept and put in order. [26] Then it goes and takes along seven other spirits more evil than itself, and they go in and live there; and the last state of that man becomes worse than the first. (Luke 11:24-26)

The devil, once he has you, will do everything he can to never let you go again. He wants to secure your soul for the kingdom of darkness.

Before we decide to follow Jesus we must count the cost. Jesus requires us to surrender all to Him, to give up everything. He makes a call for total commitment. To follow Christ, to be His disciple, we must love Christ over all things and be willing to carry our cross. If we say we want to follow Christ and we don't count the costs, we will end up being another half built tower or a casualty of war.

If you feel Jesus is asking for too much let me ask you a few of questions: (1) If you choose not to follow Christ, who are you choosing to follow? (2) If you choose not to follow Christ, do you know the blessings you are going to miss out on? (3) If you choose not to follow Christ, are you willing to pay the consequences for that decision?

God desires that you would choose Christ and live. Ezekiel 33:11 says, "Say to them, 'As I live!' declares the Lord God, 'I take no pleasure in the death of the wicked, but rather that the wicked turn from his way and live. Turn back, turn back from your evil ways! Why then will you die…?'" God is not willing that anyone would perish. He desires for us all to come to repentance (2 Peter 3:9).

The blessings and privileges of serving God far outweigh whatever suffering we endure for Christ (2 Corinthians 4:17; Romans 8:18). Jim Elliot, a missionary and martyr for Christ, once said "He is no fool who gives what he cannot keep to gain what he cannot lose."[9] Jesus said, "**24** For whoever wishes to save his life will lose it, but whoever loses his life for My sake, he is the one who will save it. **25** For what is a man profited if he gains the whole world, and loses or forfeits himself?" (Luke 9:24-25).

My desire is that you would choose Christ, that you would be willing to walk His narrow path; and that you would be willing to love Him above everyone else, above yourself, and above material possessions. Christ is worth it all. He gave His life for you. Won't you give up yours for Him?

Whatever you choose to do, just make sure you have first counted the cost.

---

[9] Roberts Liardon, *God's Generals: Martyrs* (New Kensington, PA: Whitaker House, 2016), 341.

Chapter 3
WHAT KIND OF DISCIPLE DO YOU WANT TO BE?

At this point, if you are still reading then you must be serious about wanting to follow Christ. And so the next question that you want to ask yourself is, "what kind of disciple do I want to be?"

According to Matthew 13, Jesus tells us that there are four types of people who listen to His messages and words. And since being a disciple involves obeying His teachings, you must decide what kind of disciple you want to be. Allow me to tell you up front, there is only one right answer, one right choice and three wrong ones. So choose wisely.

In Matthew 13:1-9 we see, once again, a crowd forms around Jesus. They want to hear Him speak. So in order to be heard by all, Jesus hops into a boat and spoke the following parable to the people on the shore of the beach. Jesus said,

> [3] ...Behold, the sower went out to sow; [4] and as he sowed, some seeds fell beside the road, and the birds came and ate them up. [5] Others fell on the rocky places, where they did not have much soil; and immediately they sprang up, because they had no depth of soil. [6] But when the sun had risen, they were scorched; and because they had no root, they withered away. [7] Others fell among the thorns, and the thorns came up and choked them out. [8] And others fell on the good soil and yielded a crop,

some a hundredfold, some sixty, and some thirty. ⁹ He who has ears, let him hear. (vv3-9)

Now, if you don't understand exactly what Jesus meant don't worry. Neither did the multitudes nor His disciples (Mark 4:10). Thankfully, He went on to explain what this parable meant.

¹⁸ Hear then the parable of the sower. ¹⁹ When anyone hears the word of the kingdom and does not understand it, the evil *one* comes and snatches away what has been sown in his heart. This is the one on whom seed was sown beside the road. ²⁰ The one on whom seed was sown on the rocky places, this is the man who hears the word and immediately receives it with joy; ²¹ yet he has no *firm* root in himself, but is *only* temporary, and when affliction or persecution arises because of the word, immediately he falls away. ²² And the one on whom seed was sown among the thorns, this is the man who hears the word, and the worry of the world and the deceitfulness of wealth choke the word, and it becomes unfruitful. ²³ And the one on whom seed was sown on the good soil, this is the man who hears the word and understands it; who indeed bears fruit and brings forth, some a hundredfold, some sixty, and some thirty. (vv18-23)

Now, we're able to see more clearly what Jesus wanted to communicate. In the midst of all the multitude that surrounded Him people might have thought, "Wow, Jesus is very popular. He has so many disciples!" But Jesus was actually saying, "Nope. Not everyone who is here is truly with me." The parable was to illustrate this fact.

The farmer represents Jesus. The seed He sows represents His teachings and words. The different grounds actually represent different people, hearts, and listeners. The first type of person in the multitude that is around Jesus doesn't really understand His message. The enemy easily removes the word that was planted into their heart. That person quits before they even get started.

The second listener actually takes Jesus' words to heart. They believe the message and receive it gladly. They choose to forsake all and follow Jesus. One would think this person is serious about their walk with Christ. I mean, just look at them. They are passionate and enthusiastic. They're sharing their testimony and the good news of Jesus. But they never get deep with God. They don't spend time in the Bible or in prayer. They never grow roots in their relationship with God.

Within a short period of time their loyalty and commitment to Christ is tested. Persecution arises because of their relationship to Jesus. Difficulties begin to surround them since the culture and morals of the kingdom of God are in opposition to the culture and morals of this world. Their fleshly desires begin to clash with their spiritual goals. Finally, the pressure builds up and they can no longer hold on. They give up and walk away.

This second person was genuine in their decision, but not committed enough to discipline their self and dig deep into God.

The third type of person in the multitude actually makes it a little further than the previous one. They actually go to church and Sunday School. They are present in the activities and ministries. They learn to pray and study the Bible. But their heart and attention are divided. They want to be friends with God, but they also want to be friends with the world. They want the pleasures and comforts that riches can provide. They don't want to be poor or content. Plus, they have a family to feed. So this person chooses to be content with a form of godliness but deny its power. They become lukewarm and religious. They're still present in the church but their mind is elsewhere. They are going through the motions physically, but their heart is on getting back to the "real world". They become unfruitful.

The last type of person in the crowd following Jesus represents those who hear the gospel and the message of the kingdom, believe it and receive it. They count the costs of what it would mean to follow Jesus and decide to follow Him no matter what. They dive into His word, they spend time in prayer. They seek ways to keep themselves pure and undefiled by this world. They choose to stand for Christ even when it's not popular, even when it costs them persecution and shame and rejection from the people they love. Their hearts and minds are single. They are determined, disciplined, and dedicated.

This last listener, this last person is the true disciple. This is the one who bears fruit. Some might bear more fruit than others, but they're fruitful nonetheless.

My testimony

I came to faith in Christ on November 14, 2004, at the age of seventeen. Before that I had known poverty, been exposed to domestic violence, drug trafficking, pornography, prostitution, and different kinds of sexual immorality. At the age of fifteen, I attempted suicide and then again at sixteen. I was depressed for many years. I had such a low self-esteem, that many times I would look into the mirror and literally say, "I hate you. You're so ugly."

During my senior year in high school, a friend of mine, Esther Blanco, invited me to church several times. I would say "yes" and never go until I decided to go for a youth campaign service. I went once and liked it. So I went again for a Sunday service. The preacher was a man named David Martinez. He preached a message that I still remember till this day, "Exalting the Name of Jesus." At the end of his message he made an altar call, "If you want to exalt the name of Jesus, come forward."

During the whole message, I was crying and I didn't know why. I responded to the altar call and went forward. I didn't know what I was doing but I began to close my eyes and lift my hands. I began to pray over and over, "Jesus, I want to exalt you." I didn't pray the sinner's prayer or repent of my sins. I was completely captivated by Jesus and wanted to live for Him and exalt Him for the rest of my life.

All of a sudden, I felt this immense gravity come upon me. It was pulling me down but I resisted. In my head I didn't understand what was going on and I wasn't about to get on the floor in front of all these people that I didn't even know. What would they think? But the weight got heavier and heavier. The more I resisted, the lower to the ground I got. When I was finally on one knee unable to resist anymore, I gave in. I fell flat on to the floor. I was prostrate, lying completely on the ground.

I began crying and sobbing uncontrollably. I felt "waves of liquid love" going up and down, up and down

29

my whole body. I was instantly filled with the Holy Spirit and I felt more love in that moment than I ever did in my whole life. My parents were good parents who loved me. I had a great family. But this surpassed anything I could ever imagine.

When I finally got up from the floor, I was a new person. I still had many struggles that I had to work through but within a couple of weeks I was on fire. I started devouring my Bible. I would sometimes skip school to read the Bible. I would try to leave early or arrive home as quickly as possible just so that I could pray. I would pray between three and six hours a day. I read the New Testament in two months and within one year I had read the Old Testament once and the New Testament twice. I had memorized scores of Bible verses.

Within my first two months, I was made the youth director. In my first message, five of my own family members came to Christ. I began witnessing, praying and winning souls to Christ in my high school. I started ministering in Promesa, a drug rehabilitation center, preaching the gospel to recovering addicts. I got involved in street preaching, cleaning my church, and began serving in any way I could.

I could go on and on with everything that happened to me after I committed my life to Christ. But I just want to focus on one thing which is relevant to this chapter. During that first year, when I read through the Bible, I remember reading the parable I have been speaking about. I got so scared because I thought I could be that second type of listener. I was joyful, passionate, and enthusiastic. I would pray saying, "Oh no. Please God. I don't want to be like that second ground. I want to bear much fruit for you." I literally prayed those same words, almost every day, for almost a year!

Then I decided I would not only pray about it, I would also do something about it. And by the grace of God I am still here today, serving Jesus, with passion, with enthusiasm, and still madly in love with Jesus. He is my whole world. I disciplined myself to read the Word every day and pray every day. My goal is to draw closer to Him and be able to exalt Him in whatever I do and wherever I go.

Your choice

What about you? What are you going to choose? Who are you going to be? Distractions will abound, but we are called to "fix our eyes on Jesus" (Hebrews 12:2). Persecutions will arise. The Bible says, "Indeed, all who desire to live godly in Christ Jesus will be persecuted" (2 Timothy 3:12). But if you suffer for Christ you will be blessed (Matthew 5:10-12). If you endure for Him you will reign with Him one day (2 Timothy 2:12). Let me tell you that "to live is Christ and to die is gain" (Philippians 1:21).

God desires for you to be a fruitful disciple but He cannot force you to be one. Are you going to let the devil steal His word out of your heart? Will you be the type of follower who is emotionally a fan of Jesus but never gets committed and because of that you will fall away when things get difficult? Will you get sidetracked and follow worldly pursuits while religiously claiming to be a follower of Jesus? Or will you grow deep roots and plant yourself in Christ in order to bear much fruit?

It's your choice. What kind of disciple do you want to be?

YOUR LIFE AS A DISCIPLE:
FOLLOWING IN THE
FOOTSTEPS OF JESUS

Chapter 4
YOU MUST BE BORN AGAIN

In 2013, I went through the Gospels and tracked the life of Jesus. In the following chapters of this section, I want to use the different stages and moments of Jesus' life to illustrate, or demonstrate, how we should live if we desire to follow in His footsteps.

The story of the incarnate Christ on this earth begins with His virgin birth. Isaiah prophesied hundreds of years before His birth, "For a child will be born to us, a son will be given to us" (Isaiah 9:6a) and "Behold, a virgin will be with child and bear a son, and she will call His name Immanuel" (Isaiah 7:14), "which translated means 'God with us'" (Matthew 1:23). This promise came to pass through a young virgin woman named Mary.

> [26] Now in the sixth month the angel Gabriel was sent from God to a city in Galilee called Nazareth, [27] to a virgin engaged to a man whose name was Joseph, of the descendants of David; and the virgin's name was Mary. [28] And coming in, he said to her, "Greetings, favored one! The Lord *is* with you." [29] But she was very perplexed at *this* statement, and kept pondering what kind of salutation this was. [30] The angel said to her, "Do not be afraid, Mary; for you have found favor with God. [31] And behold, you will conceive in your womb and bear a son, and you shall name Him Jesus. [32] He will be great and will be called the Son of the Most High; and the Lord God will give Him the throne of His

father David; [33] and He will reign over the house of Jacob forever, and His kingdom will have no end." [34] Mary said to the angel, "How can this be, since I am a virgin?" [35] The angel answered and said to her, "The Holy Spirit will come upon you, and the power of the Most High will overshadow you; and for that reason the holy Child shall be called the Son of God. [36] And behold, even your relative Elizabeth has also conceived a son in her old age; and she who was called barren is now in her sixth month. [37] For nothing will be impossible with God." [38] And Mary said, "Behold, the bond slave of the Lord; may it be done to me according to your word." And the angel departed from her. (Luke 1:26-38)

Now, I want us to fast forward to a very important conversation Jesus had with someone later on in His life. We will come back to the story of the virgin birth and see how it relates.

John tells us that a Pharisee named Nicodemus, "who was a ruler of the Jews" and a teacher of Israel, came to Jesus at night to speak with Him (John 3:1-2, 10). In other words, a very trained and well-learned teacher and leader of the Sanhedrin came to Jesus to inquire of spiritual things. Without beating around the bush, Jesus spoke immediately about the most pressing issue. He told Nicodemus, "Truly, truly, I say to you, unless one is born again he cannot see the kingdom of God" (John 3:3).

Now Nicodemus was confused by Jesus' words, and needing further clarification, he asked Him how this was possible. "How can a man be born when he is old? He cannot enter a second time into his mother's womb and be born, can he?" (John 3:4). Jesus responded, "⁵ ...Truly, truly, I say to you, unless one is born of water and the Spirit he cannot enter into the kingdom of God. ⁶ That which is born of the flesh is flesh, and that which is born of the Spirit is spirit" (John 3:5-6).

From the dialogue which took place between Jesus and Nicodemus we learn some valuable lessons. (1) We cannot be saved, "see the kingdom of God," unless we are born again. (2) This birth isn't a natural birth, it is a spiritual birth. It is a supernatural transformation of life that can only be accomplished by the Spirit of God. The flesh gives birth to flesh, or in other words, the natural human body can only produce natural human children. But the Spirit of God produces spiritual life and births spiritual children.

Now, "how does this relate to Jesus' virgin birth?" I am glad you asked. In the story of Mary we see that the angel, Gabriel, gives her a message. After Mary believed that message and surrendered to the will of God for her life, the Spirit of God came upon her and overshadowed her (Luke 1:35). This combination of God's message + Mary's faith and surrender + the Spirit of God coming upon her with power produced the fulfillment of God's promise; the miraculous birth of His only begotten Son.

In a similar way, when we hear God's message, the gospel, and we believe it and are willing to surrender our lives to the will of God, the Holy Spirit will enter us and give birth to the nature of Christ in us. Peter says, we become "partakers of the divine nature" (2 Peter 1:4). Paul says, that we become new creatures (2 Corinthians 5:17) and Christ begins to live within us (Galatians 2:20).

Don't be fooled by what you see on the outside. If you have surrendered your life to Jesus, you have been born again. Everything old has passed away and everything has become new (2 Corinthians 5:17). As you renew your thinking through the word of God and cooperate with the Holy Spirit, He will manifest publicly what is on the inside (Romans 12:2). This public manifestation is called the fruit of the Spirit (Galatians 5:22-23). He will help conform your life to the image of Jesus (Romans 8:29).

Before this supernatural birth, we are dead on the inside (Ephesians 2:1), which means our human spirits are "disconnected" from God. There is no relationship and no fellowship between us and God (Isaiah 59:2; Romans 3:23; 6:23a). But just as an electronic device receives power once it's connected to electricity, our human spirits receive spiritual life when we are "reconnected" with the Holy Spirit. We receive eternal life, which is a relationship with God that endures forever.

The miracle of the virgin birth can never be repeated. It happened once in order to birth our Messiah. We don't become God. But this physical event illustrates the spiritual principle of our need to be born again.[10] Christ will live in us through the Holy Spirit. We will see evidence of this through the fruits that begin to manifest in our lives. He will

---

[10] I want to make something very clear. I do not believe Christ was "born again." He didn't have a sinful nature and He never sinned therefore there was no need for Him to be born again. I am using His virgin birth as an illustration of what must occur in us spiritually.

38

work with us to conform our lives to the image of Jesus.

If we want to follow in the footsteps of Jesus then we must begin where it all began for Him. We must begin with His virgin birth. We must be born again.

Chapter 5
IDENTITY: KNOW WHO YOU ARE

If we are to follow in the footsteps of Jesus, we must know who we are. The truth contained in this chapter cannot be overemphasized. Knowing who you are and what God has made available to you will be the fountain from which all other springs will flow.

Jesus knew who He was from a very early age. Though not much information is contained in the Gospels (Matthew, Mark, Luke and John) about His life until He publicly appeared to the world, an interesting event occurred when Jesus was 12 years old.

After leaving Jerusalem from celebrating the Passover, a Jewish holiday,[11] Mary and Joseph (Jesus' mother and stepfather) lost sight of Jesus and frantically searched for Him for three days. When they found Him and questioned Him these were His words, "Why is it that you were looking for Me? Did you not know that I had to be in **My Father's** *house*?" (Luke 2:49; emphasis mine). As you can see, from a very early age, Jesus was aware of who He was and where He belonged.

At the age of 30, Jesus went to be baptized (submerged) in water by His relative, John. When Jesus came out of the water a voice from Heaven spoke and confirmed that Jesus was the Son of God and that God Himself was very pleased with Him (Matthew 3:17). This is amazing! Before Jesus ever did a miracle, before Jesus ever healed a single person, before Jesus ever casted out one demon or saved one soul; God was already pleased with

---

[11] see Exodus 12

Him just because He was His son.

It was this awareness that formed the strong foundation from which Jesus did everything else in His life. Satan knew this and after Jesus' baptism, the very first thing Satan attacked when He tempted Jesus in the desert was His identity. Twice he began his temptations with the words "If you are the Son of God" (Matthew 4:3, 6). If he could get Jesus to doubt what God had just said about Him, he would be able to trap Him. But Jesus didn't even stutter and He demolished Satan's temptations with the word of His Father!

In the same way, if the enemy can get you to doubt who you are or to be ignorant of who you are, he will keep you in bondage to things that God has already set you free from! As you read through the Bible you will learn all the wonderful things God says about who you are and what He has given to you. But there will always be the strong temptation to compare what God says about you with what you are experiencing in your life. You will be tempted to believe your experience instead of God's word. It's a lie! Don't believe your experience, don't believe Satan's voice. Believe God's word! He is not a liar!

What you believe about yourself will greatly influence how you live. What you believe about yourself will greatly impact or limit your potential in the Lord. Proverbs 23:7 says, "For as he thinks within himself, so he is." Your identity rests heavily on how you perceive yourself. Jesus says, "For the mouth speaks out of that which fills the heart" (Matthew 12:34). In other words, you will speak and you will behave in accordance to what is in your heart. Your words and your behavior are actually indications of what's going on inside of you.

This is the reason why Solomon says, "Watch over your heart with all diligence, For from it *flow* the springs of life" (Proverbs 4:23). It is important for you to guard your heart from information, words, images, or ideas that are contrary to what God has spoken over your life. Whatever you allow into your heart will become a part of how you think and how you see yourself. This in turn will produce words, behaviors, and attitudes that agree with what you believe about yourself. Life springs or flows from whatever is in your heart.

Many of us have been influenced by the words spoken to us by our parents, families, and peers. Some have cursed us with words like "you're stupid," "you will never be good enough," "you're ugly," "you're too fat," "you're too skinny," "you will always be poor," or "no one will ever love you." These words, in some cases, have become self-fulfilling prophecies or clouds of invisible forces that limit our progress and success. You might even feel these things are true because you see them as a reality in your daily experiences.

But that is not who you are. We need to renew our minds with what God says about us. We must get into His word and change the way we think and the way we view ourselves. We must replace the old, worldly, carnal, and demonic thoughts pushed upon us by the world around us with God's thoughts and words. Only then will we be able to walk freely into all that God has destined for us. You are whoever God says you are. Nothing less, nothing more. Period.

Here are just a couple of the many good things God says about you: (1) If you have humbled yourself as a child, turned away from and confessed your sins, and believe in

Jesus then you are **a son of God** (Mark 1:15; John 1:12; Romans 10:9-10). (2) If you have surrendered your life to Jesus then you have been **born again**, you have been made a **new creation**. Everything old has passed away, and everything has become new! (John 3; 2 Corinthians 5:17). (3) You will **never be alone** because **Jesus will always be with you** since the **Holy Spirit lives in you** (Matthew 28:20; John 14:17-18). (4) You will be able to **do the things Jesus did, and even greater** (John 14:12; Mark 16:15-18).

These are only a few things God says about you. I want to challenge you to begin to seek out everything the Bible says about who you are and what God has made available to you through Jesus. Here is something to keep in mind, *to the extent that you know, believe and walk in truth, to that extent will you be free, live it and see it become a reality* (John 8:31-32; Romans 12:2).

On this journey of becoming Christlike you must follow in His footsteps. His second footprint can be found in the word "Identity." Follow this step and you will be heading in the right direction.

Chapter 6
DO THE WILL OF GOD

I have never camped in the woods, much less ever gotten lost without knowing how to return back home. For years, prior to the invention of the G.P.S., many have used the North Star, also known as Polaris, which sits almost directly above the North Pole, to guide their way home or to other destinations. Knowing where North is located allows the traveler, or the person who is lost, to determine where South, East and West are. The North Star serves as a reference point to determine where one should go.

Jesus' "North Star" was the will of His Father. The will of God was His focus, His guide and His reference on how to live, where to go, what to say and what to do. Jesus came to earth to do the will of God, plain and simple. Nothing else occupied His time or agenda. Yes, He wanted to save the lost. Yes, He wanted to heal the sick. Yes, He wanted to preach to the poor. But the reason He wanted to do any of this was because it was the Father's will that He save, heal, preach and even die on a cross.

Just listen to the place and priority the will of God had in Jesus' life. "For I have come down from heaven, not to do My own will, but the will of Him who sent Me" (John 6:38). "Jesus said to them, 'My food is to do the will of Him who sent Me and to accomplish His work'" (John 4:34). "Truly, truly, I say to you, the Son can do nothing of Himself, unless *it is* something He sees the Father doing; for whatever the Father does, these things the Son also does in like manner" (John 5:19). "My Father, if it is possible, let this cup pass from Me; yet not as I will, but as You will" (Matthew 26:39).

From His birth, to His baptism, to His death; Jesus sought to do the will of God and obey His Father. Doing His Father's will was on Jesus' mind from sunup to sundown, from sunrise to sunset.

What about you? Does knowing and doing the will of God consume your thoughts? Does it drive your life and control your time? Every day, when you wake up, are you fulfilling God's agenda or yours?

Jesus taught His disciples to pray, "Your kingdom come. *Your will be done*, On earth as it is in heaven" (Matthew 6:10; emphasis mine). This was to be a daily petition as can be seen in His words, "[11] Give us *this day* our *daily* bread. [12] 'And forgive us our debts..." (6:11-12: emphasis mine). We ask God for provision and for forgiveness on a daily basis, don't we? In the same way, we must ask for God's kingdom to come and His will to be done daily. God's kingdom and His will come together in one package.

Now, notice the words "earth" and "heaven" in this petition. Who is in heaven and who is on earth? God is in heaven and you are on earth. Whenever we pray this prayer we're asking for God to accomplish His will in our lives. We're asking for Him to govern us, reign over us, and to be in charge over our lives. In the same way God governs and reigns in heaven and His will is always done by the saints and angels, so on earth we should desire to see His will done in others, but even more specifically, in ourselves.

Look at the advantage of doing God's will. John says, "The world is passing away, and *also* its lusts; but the one who does the will of God lives forever" (1 John 2:17). In contrast to the fashions and fads of this world, the person who does God's will, will never die or fade away. Let me tell you that the safest place on earth is in the perfect will of God. He will never lead you astray. He will always have your best in mind (Jeremiah 29:11). Even when His will leads you through the valley of the shadow of death, His presence, protection and provision will always go with you (Psalm 23:4).

The will of God must take center place in your life if you are to become like Jesus. Jesus Himself said, "But seek first His kingdom and His righteousness, and all these things will be added to you" (Matthew 6:33). Now, when Jesus says that we should seek His kingdom "first," He is saying that we should seek it "first" in terms of chronology and "first" in terms of priority. Chronology has to do with time. Priority has to do with importance. Let me explain this a little more.

To seek His kingdom first, chronologically, means to seek His will before you seek anything else. Before you start your day, you should desire to seek and do God's will for your life. Before making any important decisions with your life, you should desire to seek and do the will of God for your life. Before you chose to get into any relationship, you should desire to seek and do the will of God for your life. No matter what you say, or people say, God should have the first and the last word.

Now, to seek His kingdom first, in terms of priority, is a reference to importance. We must see His kingdom and His will as more important and more valuable to us than anything or anyone else. "For where your treasure is, there your heart will be also" (Matthew 6:21). Can I tell you that your heart will desire, your heart will seek; you will make sacrifices for whatever you think is valuable?

What is God's will for your life? What is He asking you to do? Set your heart and mind today on discovering what the will of God is for your life in general (long term) and specifically (daily). Align yourself with God. By knowing and obeying God's will, you will walk in a manner worthy of the Lord, you will please *Him* in all aspects, you will bear fruit in every good work and increase in the knowledge of God (Colossians 1:10).

Jesus says that those who do the will of God are blessed (Luke 11:28), which means happy, fortunate, favored by God, receiver of God's benefits, and someone to be envied.[12] He also calls those who do the will of God His own brothers, sisters, and mothers (Mark 3:35).

If you wonder if it's even possible to know God's will that clearly Paul says, "And do not be conformed to this world, but be transformed by the renewing of your mind, so that you may prove what the will of God is, that which is good and acceptable and perfect" (Romans 12:2). In other words, if you will refuse to think and act like the world, and if you will change the way you think by getting into God's word and spending time with Him in prayer, you will be able to know what is God's good, acceptable, and perfect will.

Kathryn Kuhlman used to say, "The Heavenly Father does not ask for golden vessels. He does not ask for silver vessels. God asks for yielded vessels – those who will submit their will to the will of the Father. And the greatest human attainment in all the world is for a life to be so surrendered to Him that the name of God Almighty will be glorified through that life."

---

[12] Strong's #3107

We need to become Christlike. This involves following in His footsteps and if the will of God was Jesus' focus, guide and North Star, shouldn't it be ours?

Chapter 7
MISSION: ESTABLISHING THE KINGDOM OF GOD

When God created mankind in His image and likeness, His intention was for man to rule and have dominion over the whole earth (Genesis 1:26). When man sinned, his image became corrupt and depraved like God's enemy, thus his authority was handed over to God's enemy - Satan (Luke 4:6). Since that time Satan has tried to reshape the world in his image. He has established his own perverted and dark kingdom (Ephesians 6:18). He has tried to persecute, distort, and kill everything and everyone that looks like God in this world. He has attempted to infiltrate and sabotage God's people and God's work.[13] He has set himself up as the god of this world (2 Corinthians 4:4) and has brought people under his power (1 John 5:19) through fear and deception (Hebrews 2:15; John 8:44).

But when Christ came to the earth, He came to undo everything Satan had done (1 John 3:8). He came to usher in the authority, the rule, the dominion, the government of God - the kingdom of God! For that reason the very first message Jesus began to proclaim was "The time is fulfilled, and the kingdom of God is at hand; repent and believe in the gospel" (Mark 1:15). He would begin to take back what the devil had deceitfully stolen. This surely is good news.

During His lifetime, Jesus demonstrated that God was once again taking over by the casting out of demons. "But if I cast out demons by the Spirit of God, then the kingdom of God has come upon you" (Matthew 12:28). He

---

[13] See the parable of the tares among the wheat in Matthew 13:24-30, 36-43.

would also do this by healing the sick (Acts 10:38; Luke 13:16), and by preaching this good news to the poor (7:20-22). "¹⁸ The Spirit of the Lord is upon Me, Because He anointed Me to preach the gospel to the poor. He has sent Me to proclaim release to the captives, And recovery of sight to the blind, To set free those who are oppressed, ¹⁹ To proclaim the favorable year of the Lord" (Luke 4:18-19).

Through His death and resurrection Jesus has disarmed Satan, and completely defeated death and the grave (Hebrews 2:14-15; Colossians 2:15; Revelation 1:18). When Jesus returns to the earth, He will establish a physical kingdom as prophesied by Daniel,

> ¹³ I kept looking in the night visions, and behold, with the clouds of heaven one like a Son of Man was coming, and He came up to the Ancient of Days and was presented before Him. ¹⁴ "And to Him was given dominion, glory and a kingdom, that all the peoples, nations and *men of every* language might serve Him. His dominion is an everlasting dominion which will not pass away; and His kingdom is one which will not be destroyed. (7:13-14)

After this He will ultimately remove Satan, death, sickness, pain, and the curse from this world (Rev. 20:10, 14; 21:1, 3-4).

The kingdom of God was Jesus' message and it was the message His followers were to preach and demonstrate. The king had come to reign and it is His desire to rule *in* the hearts of men before He rules *over* the nations with an iron rod. God allowed the world to go its own way for some time, but now He commands that all men repent (Acts 17:30). "For he has set a day when he will judge the world with justice by the man he has appointed. He has given proof of this to everyone by raising him from the dead" (Acts 17:31).

Jesus promised to be with all believers and give them power as they took on this Great Commission (Matthew 28:18-20; Mark 16:15-18; Acts 1:8). He told His followers to go from town to town and cast out devils, heal the sick, and preach the kingdom of God (Luke 9:1-2; 10:8-9). This commission, this task, this demonstration and this message is not an option. It is not for a special group of Christians. It is not for full-time pastors, evangelists, teachers, or ministers. EVERY FOLLOWER OF JESUS MUST ESTABLISH HIS KINGDOM HERE ON THE EARTH! We are to make disciples as Jesus made disciples and we are to teach them to obey everything that He has commanded.

So as we go to work or school and live our daily lives, we are to reach out to those around us (family, friends, coworkers, and strangers). We are to inform them of who Jesus is and what He has done for them. We are to persuade them to turn from evil and give their lives over to God because He loves them, died to forgive them, and wants to fulfill His purpose in them. Those who choose to trust God will be forgiven of all their wrongs (Luke 24:46-47), will be made a brand new person (John 3:3; 2 Corinthians 5:17), will become a true child of God (John 1:12), and will enjoy a never-ending relationship with God in this life and the one to come (John 17:3; 11:25-26; Romans 8:28-39). And coupled together with your message, you can confirm and demonstrate this message by healing the sick, delivering those in bondage to the devil, by living a transformed life and by showing them God's unconditional love (Acts 10:38).

The more people turn to God, the bigger His kingdom becomes, the more the earth is filled with God's glory, and the quicker we will usher in the coming of Christ and the renewal of all things (Matthew 24:14). His people are to become like yeast. "The kingdom of heaven is like leaven, which a woman took and hid in three pecks of flour until it was all leavened" (Matthew 13:33). Nebuchadnezzar saw this in a dream,

> [34] You continued looking until a stone was cut out without hands, and it struck the statue on its feet of iron and clay and crushed them. [35] Then the iron, the clay, the bronze, the silver and the gold were crushed all at the same time and became like chaff from the summer threshing floors; and the wind carried them away so that not a trace of them was found. But the stone that struck the statue became a great mountain and filled the whole earth... [44] In the days of those kings the God of heaven will set up a kingdom which will never be destroyed, and *that* kingdom will not be left for another people; it will crush and put an end to all these kingdoms, but it will itself endure forever. [45] Inasmuch as you saw that a stone was cut out of the mountain without hands and that it crushed the iron, the bronze, the clay, the silver and the gold, the great God has made known to the king what will take place in the future; so the

dream is true and its interpretation is trustworthy. (Daniel 2:34-35, 44-45)

If we are truly going to become Christlike and follow in His footsteps, we must dedicate our lives to fulfilling His mission. We are the body of Christ here on the earth. And His mission is to establish the kingdom of God in this world.

Chapter 8
BE FILLED WITH THE SPIRIT: A LIFE OF POWER

Not much is known about the life of Jesus before the day He was baptized in water.[14] All four Gospels focus more on what He did beginning with the day He came up out of the water and the Holy Spirit came upon Him like a dove. It was not until He was anointed, singled out and empowered by the Holy Spirit that His real work on the earth began.

Peter described what happened to Jesus with these words, *"You know of* Jesus of Nazareth, how God anointed Him with the Holy Spirit and with power, and *how* He went about doing good and healing all who were oppressed by the devil, for God was with Him"* (Acts 10:38).

Until the day that He was baptized in water and anointed by the Holy Spirit, Jesus could do no miracles, signs, or wonders. But once the Holy Spirit came upon Him, Jesus received power. He healed all the sick who came to Him. He casted out demons from those who were oppressed by the devil. He raised the dead, opened the eyes of the blind, cured the lepers, revealed the secrets of people's lives, was given extraordinary wisdom, and proclaimed the kingdom of God. Another one of His followers even said, "Jesus did many other things as well. If every one of them were written down, I suppose that even the whole world would not have room for the books that would be written" (John 21:25). Wow! Amazing!

---

[14] See Matthew 1-2; Luke 1-3 for more information on the life of Jesus before His baptism.

Now, you might be wondering "if Jesus was God why did He need the Holy Spirit to come upon Him in order to begin to do supernatural things?"

We must remember that Jesus was God wrapped in human flesh (John 1:1, 14). When Jesus became a man He emptied Himself of all His power and glory (Philippians 2:6-7). He became just like any ordinary man with the exception that He did not sin (Hebrews 2:17-18; 4:15). He was still God. He was still one with the Father. But in humbling Himself, He took on the limitations of a man - He aged, He hungered, He thirst, He bled.

There are many reasons why Jesus needed to become like this. One of the primary reasons, most relevant to the topic of this chapter, is that Jesus was setting an example for you and me. He was demonstrating what you and I would be able to do as normal human beings anointed and empowered by the Spirit of God. If Jesus did anything as God, we could not follow His example. We would say, "Well, of course Jesus could do that, He was God!"[15] But the very fact that Jesus walked as a normal human being that couldn't do any miracles until the Spirit was upon Him is a lesson to us that we too can do what Jesus did.

Jesus commands His followers to be filled and empowered by the same Spirit He possessed so that we could not only do the same things He did, but even greater things than He did! (John 14:12). Jesus told His disciples that before they were to go into all the world and preach the gospel they were to "stay in the city until you are clothed with power from on high" (Luke 24:49). "⁴ He commanded

---

[15] Don't we already say things like that when we try to imitate His example in living a righteous life? "Of course, Jesus didn't sin. He was God. I am just a man." Even this idea is erroneous.

them not to leave Jerusalem, but to wait for what the Father had promised, 'Which,' He said, 'you heard of from Me; ⁵ for John baptized with water, but you will be baptized with the Holy Spirit not many days from now'" (Acts 1:4-5). Once they received this baptism they would "receive power when the Holy Spirit has come upon you; and you shall be My witnesses both in Jerusalem, and in all Judea and Samaria, and even to the remotest part of the earth" (Acts 1:8).

Can you see why it is so important that we be filled with the Holy Spirit? Notice that His disciples would be His witnesses only after the Holy Spirit came upon them and they received power from on high. This power would enable them to move in the supernatural. Now, before you begin to think that this command was only for the Apostles and the early church I want you to read the words of Mark. He says,

> ¹⁵ And He said to them, "Go into all the world and preach the gospel to all creation. ¹⁶ He who has believed and has been baptized shall be saved; but he who has disbelieved shall be condemned. ¹⁷ These signs will accompany those who have believed: in My name they will cast out demons, they will speak with new tongues; ¹⁸ they will pick up serpents, and if they drink any deadly *poison*, it will not hurt them; they will lay hands on the sick, and they will recover." (16:15-18)

The promise is for all who "have believed." This promise is in the context of the Great Commission, which is for all Christians.

Without this power we cannot be effective witnesses for Christ.[16] "The kingdom of God is not a matter of talk but of power" (1 Corinthians 4:20). We are not to depend on our wisdom, eloquence, talents or charisma to testify about Jesus but on God's power so that when people believe, their "faith will not rest on man's wisdom but on God's power" (1 Corinthians 2:1-5). Adrian Rogers used to say, "Anything that I can argue you into, someone else can argue you out of! But a man with a testimony, a man who has encountered God can never be persuaded to stop believing in God" (paraphrased).[17]

This power cannot be experienced apart from the presence of the Holy Spirit. We are commanded to continuously be filled with the Spirit (Ephesians 5:18). God must work through us if we are to effectively proclaim, represent, and glorify Christ. Any work that we accomplish in our strength, in our flesh, or in our wisdom will wither up and die. But whatever is done through the power, strength and presence of God will remain forever (1 Corinthians 3:11-15).

Our motivation for seeking to be filled is not to glorify or gratify ourselves, but to exalt Christ and expand the kingdom of God! Christ, as a man filled with the Holy Spirit is our example. Examine all that He did in only three years!

If Jesus, the Son of God, needed to be filled and

---

[16] I wrote a whole book dedicated to this topic. In *Christlike: Supernatural*, you will learn how to reach the lost with the power and gifts of the Holy Spirit. This book will not only inspire you, but give you practical steps for learning how to move in the supernatural power of God. I truly believe that power evangelism was one of the primary reasons why the early church was so effective in winning the lost to Christ.

[17] See John chapter 9 for an example of this.

empowered by the Spirit; if the Apostles needed to be filled and empowered by the Spirit; if the early church needed to be filled and empowered by the Spirit, what makes us think that we could do more without it?

If we are to be Christlike, we must follow in His footsteps and be filled with the Holy Spirit in order to testify about the kingdom of God with power! He ascended into Heaven but gave us the Holy Spirit so that we could continue His work here on Earth (John 14-16). He has passed the baton on to us. We want to imitate His character and His presence. We want to imitate His fruits and His power. I encourage you to get alone with God and wrestle with Him in prayer day and night, until He blesses you with this gift (Luke 11:9-13). It is His will. It is His desire to do so.

Chapter 9
IMITATING THE PRAYER LIFE OF JESUS

If you followed Jesus around while He was still living on the earth it would not take very long to notice that He was a man of prayer. As a matter of fact, He would often get alone with His Father and speak to Him. "Jesus often withdrew to lonely places and prayed." (Luke 5:16). The more solitary, the more withdrawn, and the more private the place - the better it was.

Jesus could not let one day go by without hearing the voice, seeing the face, or feeling the presence of His Father. He loved His Father. Jesus would rise very early in the morning while it was still dark simply to be alone with God (Mark 1:35). He was never too busy to pray. As a matter of fact, the heavier His schedule was and the more important the decisions He had to make, the more He would pray. For example, He spent a whole night in prayer before choosing the 12 men that would eventually take on His work. "12 It was at this time that He went off to the mountain to pray, and He spent the whole night in prayer to God. 13 And when day came, He called His disciples to Him and chose twelve of them, whom He also named as apostles." (Luke 6:12-13).

Christ was so intimate with His Father that His prayer life was extraordinary. He would pray and the heavens would open (Luke 3:21). He would pray and His appearance would be transformed (Luke 9:28-29). He would pray and God would audibly respond (John 12:28). He would pray and angels would attend Him (Luke 22:42-44). His prayer life was so amazing that His own disciples, already familiar with seeing prayer done on a daily basis, asked Jesus to teach them how to pray! (Luke 11:1).

Now if Jesus, the Son of God needed to pray, wanted to pray and continually prayed, don't you think that we should also? If prayer was a priority in the life of Jesus, then we who are His followers should also make prayer a priority in our lives. As I have heard many say, "Don't ever get so caught up in doing the work of the Lord that you forget the Lord of the work." There is no schedule so demanding, no suffering so painful, and no trial so difficult that should cause you to sacrifice prayer! We need to get alone with God every day. We must pray continually (1 Thessalonians 5:17).

If you are ignorant on how to pray, then read what Jesus has to say. In the Sermon on the Mount Jesus taught us to first pray in secret.

> [5] When you pray, you are not to be like the hypocrites; for they love to stand and pray in the synagogues and on the street corners so that they may be seen by men. Truly I say to you, they have their reward in full. [6] But you, when you pray, go into your inner room, close your door and pray to your Father who is in secret, and your Father who sees *what is done* in secret will reward you. (Matthew 6:5-6)

The purpose of prayer isn't popularity but intimacy. We shouldn't do our private devotions to receive praise from men. We should find a place where we can be alone with God so that we would grow closer to Him. God will then cause men to see publicly what we have gained with Him privately.

Second, Jesus taught us to pray simply. "⁷ And when you are praying, do not use meaningless repetition as the Gentiles do, for they suppose that they will be heard for their many words. ⁸ So do not be like them; for your Father knows what you need before you ask Him" (Matthew 6:7-8). You do not need to use words that sound like you're reading from a dictionary or a Shakespearean play when talking to God. God just wants to hear your heart. He wants to "commune as friend with friend." Fake, long, hypocritical prayers turn Him off and causes Him to close His ear to you. Be yourself and just converse simply.

Third, follow the model of the Lord's Prayer.

⁹ Pray, then, in this way:

"Our Father who is in heaven,
Hallowed be Your name.
¹⁰ 'Your kingdom come.
Your will be done,
On earth as it is in heaven.
¹¹ 'Give us this day our daily bread.
¹² 'And forgive us our debts, as we also have
forgiven our debtors.
¹³ 'And do not lead us into temptation, but
deliver us from evil. For Yours is the
kingdom and the power and the glory
forever. Amen." (Matthew 6:9-13)

Following the model of the Lord's Prayer doesn't mean you have to quote it or repeat it over and over in vain repetition. It just means to use it as a guide on what to say. Worship, thank, and praise Him (vv9-10); present your needs to Him and make any requests (v11); confess your sins to Him (v12); pray for divine protection from evil and temptation (v13a); and lastly, end with some more worship, thanksgiving, and praise (v13b).

Some additional pieces of advice when praying is pray expecting an answer. "[7] Ask, and it will be given to you; seek, and you will find; knock, and it will be opened to you. [8] For everyone who asks receives, and he who seeks finds, and to him who knocks it will be opened" (Matthew 7:7-8). God responds to faith. Without faith you cannot please Him (Hebrews 11:6) and you cannot consistently receive answers to your prayers (James 1:6-8). If you pray according to His will, be confident that He will hear you, and if He hears you, you will receive an answer to your prayers (1 John 5:14-15).

Lastly, when it is possible pray with others (Matthew 18:19-20) and for others (Ephesians 6:18; Hebrews 13:3).

Prayer should become an endless source of joy for you. As you speak to God and He answers, your heart will rejoice in His love and care (John 16:24). Even when waiting on an answer you will still find contentment just from being in His presence (Psalm 16:11). I cannot stress enough the importance of becoming a man or woman of prayer when it comes to following Christ and becoming like Him. If you want to become Christlike you must follow in His footsteps. Beloved, Christ has left a deeply printed foot in prayer.

Chapter 10
FULL OF THE WORD

How well do you know the word of God? How important is it for you to read it, know it, and live it? The scriptures in fact had a very central role and place in the life of Jesus.

From a very early age, Jesus immersed Himself in the Scriptures, asking questions about it and giving profound answers to His audience (Luke 2:46-47). He memorized and used it to defend Himself against the temptations of Satan (Luke 4:4, 8, 12). He honored the word in the strongest of terms (Matthew 5:18-19). Whenever the opinions or traditions of men violated or overshadowed the words of God, Jesus came into sharp disagreement with them (Mark 7:6-8). He made every effort to live in such a way as to fulfill everything that was written in the scriptures and He never failed (Matthew 5:17; 13:13, 34-35; Hebrews 4:15). Jesus Himself is considered to be the living word (John 1:1, 14).

If we are to follow in the footsteps of Christ we must also make the word of God a priority in our lives. Any person who claims to be born again and has no desire to know the word of God, their salvation can be questioned. It is as natural for a born again Christian to desire the word, as it is for a new born baby to desire milk. Peter, an Apostle of Jesus Christ, said, "Like newborn babies, long for the pure milk of the word, so that by it you may grow in respect to salvation" (1 Peter 2:2). A real Christian must desire to fill themselves with the word of God.

We must read, study, memorize, internalize, and live it. The Bible gives us many reasons why. First, it is inspired by God (2 Timothy 3:16). The actual Greek word means "God-breathed." Just like when God breathed into clay and brought Adam to life, or just like when a wind blows on the sail of a boat to move it along, so God "breathed" or moved the human authors to write what they wrote. Yes, the Bible was written by men, but these men did not write what they wanted apart from God. "[20] But know this first of all, that no prophecy of Scripture is a matter of one's own interpretation, [21] for no prophecy was ever made by an act of human will, but men moved by the Holy Spirit spoke from God" (2 Peter 1:20-21).

Second, it points us in the direction of Christ and makes us wise for salvation (2 Timothy 3:15). Without God's word we would not know the way of salvation nor would we be able to fully and clearly explain it to someone else. Again Peter said, "for you have been born again not of seed which is perishable but imperishable, *that is*, through the living and enduring word of God" (1 Peter 1:23).

Third, it is able to teach us, train us, correct us, and equip us to do everything God has called us to do (2 Timothy 3:16-17). We were all created with a purpose (Ephesians 2:10) and the best way to determine that purpose and become ready to fulfill that purpose is by knowing the word of God. Through the Bible, we learn both from the good and bad examples on how to live for God and obey His will. Paul said, "For whatever was written in earlier times was written for our instruction" (Romans 15:4). He also said, "Now these things happened to them as an example, and they were written for our instruction, upon whom the ends of the ages have come" (1 Corinthians 10:11).

The fourth reason we should read, study, memorize, internalize, and live the Bible is because it is literally the bread that feeds our spirits and gives us life (John 6:63). When tempted by Satan to turn a stone into bread, Jesus responded, "It is written, 'Man shall not live on bread alone, but on every word that proceeds out of the mouth of God.'" (Matthew 4:4). What food is to our physical bodies, the word of God is to our soul and spirit.

Fifth, it gives us light and direction when we are walking in darkness and confusion. A Psalmist said, "Your word is a lamp to my feet, And a light to my path" (Psalm 119:105). There will be times when you will need guidance on a particular subject or situation. Many turn to friends when seeking advice. There isn't anything wrong with that but God wants you to first go to His word and seek His will there.

Sixth, it is the sword with which we cut down our enemy, temptation, and strongholds in our minds (Ephesians 6:17; 2 Corinthians 10:4-5). Although I mentioned it earlier, it is interesting to note that when Jesus was confronted by the devil He did not throw stones at him. He didn't curse at him, or run from him. He didn't go into deep intercession or play spiritual music. Some of these things (prayer and music) are useful, but this was not His defense. All Jesus did was quote the word of God at the devil. He submitted Himself to God's will, He resisted doing Satan's will, and He quoted God's word.

In the same way, when you face the enemy you will need to quote the Bible. But how can you quote something that you never read? That is one reason why many Christians face defeat when tempted or attacked by the devil. They don't know how to use their sword.

Seventh, it is the truth that sets us free and helps transform us into the image of God (John 8:32; Romans 12:2). The more we read the Bible and replace our old thoughts with God's word, the more we will begin to speak and live according to God's will. We will walk securely in our identity as children of God and will not be easily deceived by the father of lies.

Eighth, it is the measure by which we judge and discern what truly is from God (2 Peter 2:19-21; Galatians 1:8; Acts 17:11-12). There are so many false teachers and religions out there. One of the surest ways of defending ourselves from deception is by knowing God's word.

This brings me to the last and final reason we should read, study, memorize, internalize, and live the Bible. We are called to be workers of God who are approved by Him because we know how to handle His word (2 Timothy 2:15). We are called to teach and preach God's word (Matthew 28:20; Mark 16:15; 2 Timothy 4:2). We are called to defend what we believe (1 Peter 3:15). But beloved, how can we share, teach, or preach His word if we do not know His word? How can we defend what we believe or explain Christ to others if we do not study His word? How can we be approved by God as His workers if we do not even know how to handle His word?

Allow me to give you this warning, if you do not spend time reading, studying, memorizing and internalizing the word of God daily you will be a weak Christian; a Christian who is easily deceived by false prophets, teachers, religions, and philosophies; a Christian who will not be able to defend nor persuade others of the truth; a Christian with a weak foundation to stand up against temptations and adversity; a Christian who will not grow in his or her relationship with God. I could go on but I think you get the point.

If you want to be Christlike you must follow in His footsteps. Make the Word a priority in your life and give it the same place in your heart that Jesus gave it in His.

Chapter 11
RIGHTEOUSNESS: BEARING GOOD FRUIT

The holiest man to ever walk the earth was Jesus Christ. He was tempted in every way, just as we are, but He never gave in. He lived a sinless life and He never disobeyed God (Hebrews 4:15). Jesus was completely righteous - approved by God and in right-standing with Him. His obedient life was the outflow of a heart that was surrendered and totally in love with the Father.

Many in His day tried seeking this righteousness, this approval of God, this right-standing with God by doing good deeds and following the law and other traditions. But many of these people (Pharisees, Sadducees, experts and teachers of the law) tried doing this by an outward form of obedience. They would honor God with their lips but their hearts were far from Him (Matthew 15:8). They would fast at least twice a week and present their tithes, but pride filled their hearts (Luke 18:9-14). They gave honor to things that were far less important in the eyes of God and neglected the things God cared for the most (Matthew 23:23). Jesus describes these men as blind guides (Matthew 23:24), as vessels that are clean on the outside but are dirty on the inside (Matthew 23:25), as whitewashed tombs, snakes and vipers (Matthew 23:27, 33).

Jesus warned His followers not to imitate their behavior (Matthew 23:3). "For I tell you that unless your righteousness surpasses that of the Pharisees and the teachers of the law, you will certainly not enter the kingdom of heaven" (Matthew 5:20). But what is the type of righteousness that surpasses that of the Pharisees and the teachers of the law? It is a righteousness that begins on the inside at the time of our conversion and manifests on the outside as we progress in our relationship with God.

Understand this, all men have sinned against God and are unrighteous before Him (Romans 3:23). Every good deed we accomplish in order to win God's approval and be right with Him will in fact fall short to His standards of perfection and holiness (Isaiah 64:6). The only way to get right with God is by His grace through faith in Jesus Christ (Ephesians 2:8-9). Any man that will humble himself and surrender His life to Jesus will find peace with God (Romans 5:1). This is how we become righteous in God's eyes.

However, being made right with God is only the first step in our journey. Next, we must demonstrate that we have truly surrendered our lives to God and that we are truly followers of His son, Jesus Christ. We do this by producing fruit that gives proof we have repented of our sins and have been forgiven (Matthew 3:8; Acts 26:20; Philippians 1:27). Jesus said that "A good tree cannot bear bad fruit, and a bad tree cannot bear good fruit. Thus, by their fruit you will recognize them" (Matthew 7:18, 20).

Let's put it this way. How do you know that an apple tree is an apple tree? Because it produces apples. How do you know that an orange tree is an orange tree? Because it produces oranges. If you saw an apple tree and someone told you it was an orange tree, you would immediately correct the person. "That is not an orange tree. It is an apple tree." They might reply, "How do you know that is an apple tree and not an orange tree? Who made you a judge or an expert?" And you would probably respond, "I don't have to be an expert. I know it is not an orange tree but an apple tree because it does not have any oranges, it only has apples hanging from its branches."

In the same way, how do you know if someone has truly given their lives to Jesus? How can you tell if they are true Christians, genuine Christ followers who have been born again with His nature and His Spirit within themselves? You will know simply because they will begin to live as He lived and love as He loved. The lifestyle and character of Jesus will begin to show up in their lives.

This does not mean that the person will never sin or fall. Even good trees might produce bad apples from time to time. Nevertheless, the fruits will generally and consistently be good. Similarly, the true Christian will not live in consistent, unrepentant, willful sin. The true Christian will have a lifestyle of righteousness, obedience, and love.

Living an obedient lifestyle of not-sinning is possible but first you must deal with the inside. Everything you do is the result of what you think, feel, and desire to do in your heart (Matthew 12:34). So if you want to live a transformed life, a life that matches the life of Jesus, then begin by purifying and guarding your heart (Proverbs 4:23). Begin by renewing your mind (Romans 12:2). If you want to bear fruits that show you belong to Jesus, then let God's word get inside of you (John 15:7-8).

To renew your mind with God's word means to replace your old thoughts with new thoughts based on what the Bible says. If you see things one way and while reading the Bible you come across a verse or passage that teaches something different, make an intentional voluntary decision to believe, agree, and apply what the Bible says and abandon your own opinion and practice. This isn't always simple, especially if what you believed was an important tradition in the family, or was something you were taught or did since you were young. But it is very effective.

Before coming to the Lord, like many people, I used to curse frequently. Every other sentence I spoke had some type of profanity. This was especially true when I got angry or was arguing with someone. I also made many jokes with double meaning. After giving my life to Christ I read these two passages: "But I tell you that every careless word that people speak, they shall give an accounting for it in the day of judgment" (Matthew 12:36) and

> [8] But no one can tame the tongue; *it is* a restless evil *and* full of deadly poison. [9] With it we bless *our* Lord and Father, and with it we curse men, who have been made in the likeness of God; [10] from the same mouth come *both* blessing and cursing. My brethren, these things ought not to be this way. [11] Does a fountain send out from the same opening *both* fresh and bitter *water*? [12] Can a fig tree, my brethren, produce olives, or a vine produce figs? Nor *can* salt water produce fresh. (James 3:8-12)

It was like a punch in the gut. "God will judge me based on my words!" I felt so much conviction and fear come over me. I did not know how I would be able to abandon such a common and lifelong practice. But I couldn't unread those verses, so I decided to put them into practice. I began to memorize, repeat, and quote them regularly until it became a part of me. My thinking changed and I no longer wanted to curse or tell dirty jokes. Now, I stay away from these things and try to speak in a way that honors God. I don't always succeed, but that is no longer my lifestyle.

As you cooperate with God in working inside of you, the outside will come into alignment. Don't ever get discouraged and give up as you try to walk in righteousness like Jesus. He will never give up on you (Philippians 1:6). Following in His footsteps means you need to walk in righteousness. This is one of the greatest signs of being Christlike.

Chapter 12
BE PERFECT. BECOME LOVE.

When asked which was the greatest commandment in the Law, Jesus pointed to two specifically. "²⁹ Jesus answered, 'The foremost is, "Hear, O Israel! The Lord our God is one Lord; ³⁰ and you shall love the Lord your God with all your heart, and with all your soul, and with all your mind, and with all your strength." ³¹ The second is this, "You shall love your neighbor as yourself." There is no other commandment greater than these'" (Mark 12:29-31). The first greatest commandment had to do with loving God and the other with loving your neighbor. Everything that is written in God's word can be summed up in one word – love (Matthew 22:40; Romans 13:8-10). In other words, if we can learn to love we can literally fulfill all of the commands of God.

But what is love? Is it a sentiment or an emotion? Is it chemical elements or hormones in the human body that cause human beings to be physically attracted to one another? What exactly is love and what does it look like? How is it expressed?

Paul defines love in these words,

⁴ Love is patient, love is kind and is not jealous; love does not brag and is not arrogant, ⁵ does not act unbecomingly; it does not seek its own, is not provoked, does not take into account a wrong suffered, ⁶ does not rejoice in unrighteousness, but rejoices with the truth; ⁷ bears all things, believes all things, hopes all things, endures all things.⁸ Love

never fails; (1 Corinthians 13:4-8a)

Now, whatever you believe about love, according to the Bible you will notice that love is not merely a sentiment, although it can contain emotions. Look at all the descriptions of love: it is patient, kind, not jealous, does not brag, not arrogant, forgives, rejoices for the right reasons, bears, believes, hopes, endures, and never fails. Love is not a feeling, it is a verb; love is an action word.

I believe we could actually condense or summarize all of these biblical descriptions about love into one word – Jesus. In one of his books, Max Lucado, actually recommended doing the following exercise so that we could see how Jesus is love. Go back to the passage in 1 Corinthians 13:4-8 and insert the name of Jesus everywhere where love is described. This is what you would end up with.

> [4] *Jesus* is patient, *Jesus* is kind and is not jealous; *Jesus* does not brag and is not arrogant, [5] does not act unbecomingly; *Jesus* does not seek His own, is not provoked, does not take into account a wrong suffered, [6] does not rejoice in unrighteousness, but rejoices with the truth; [7] bears all things, believes all things, hopes all things, endures all things.[8] *Jesus* never fails; (1 Corinthians 13:4-8a; emphasis mine)

If we want to know what love is, what it looks like, and how it can be expressed, we must look to Jesus.

The Bible says, "God is love" (1 John 4:8). Jesus was and is the greatest expression of love. He came to this world because of love (John 3:16). It was out of love and compassion that Jesus healed, taught, discipled and fed the multitudes (Matthew 9:36; 14:14; 15:32; 20:34; Mark 6:34; 8:2). It was out of love that He gave His life on the cross (John 15:12-13). What impacts me the most about His sacrifice was that He did it while we were still His enemies (Romans 5:8). Till this day He loves us and nothing will ever take that love away (Romans 8:31-39). His love towards us is perfect. Nothing we do can make Him love us more and nothing we do can make Him love us less.

Now, if we are to be Christlike then we are to love as He loves (John 15:12; 1 John 4:11-12). We are called to be perfect as God is perfect (Matthew 5:48). We are to love our neighbors (Leviticus 19:18; Matthew 22:39). We are to love our brothers and sisters in Christ (1 John 3:16). And hardest, yet most important of all, we are to love our enemies (Matthew 5:44). It is when we are able to love those who hate us, hurt us, betray us, and who do not deserve to be loved that we most reflect God. It is the way of the world, the way of Satan to repay evil for evil. It is the way of the world, the way of Satan to only care for those we like and do us favors, yet hate our enemies. But it is the way of Christ, the way of God, to love our enemies, to pray for those who persecute us and to bless those who curse us (Matthew 5:43-47).

If we were to look at the context of Jesus' command to be perfect as He is perfect, we would see that it is found in the context of loving people who are different from us, especially if they are our enemies. We are called to love all men even when all men do not love us. Jesus said,

> [43] "You have heard that it was said, 'You shall love your neighbor and hate your enemy.' [44] But I say to you, love your enemies and pray

> for those who persecute you, ⁴⁵ so that you may be sons of your Father who is in heaven; for He causes His sun to rise on *the* evil and *the* good, and sends rain on *the* righteous and *the* unrighteous. ⁴⁶ For if you love those who love you, what reward do you have? Do not even the tax collectors do the same? ⁴⁷ If you greet only your brothers, what more are you doing *than others*? Do not even the Gentiles do the same? ⁴⁸ ***Therefore you are to be perfect, as your heavenly Father is perfect***. (Matthew 5:43-48; emphasis mine)

Do you understand that love is the greatest weapon in the arsenal of a Christian? It is awesome to have great faith, to move mountains, to prophesy and understand great mysteries, to see miracles and even give your life for the poor. But without love all of those things are meaningless (1 Corinthians 13:1-3). Love is the greatest virtue in the world (1 Corinthians 13:13). It "always protects, always trusts, always hopes, always perseveres. Love never fails" (1 Corinthians 13:7-8a).

Do you want to know if you are growing in love or are being perfected in love? Let's re-do Max Lucado's exercise, but this time insert your name wherever love is being described.

> ⁴ ____ is patient, ____ is kind and is not jealous; ____ does not brag and is not arrogant, ⁵ does not act unbecomingly; ____ does not seek His own, is not provoked, does not take into account a wrong suffered, ⁶ does not rejoice in unrighteousness, but rejoices with the truth; ⁷ bears all things, believes all

things, hopes all things, endures all things.[8]
____ never fails; (1 Corinthians 13:4-8a)

Jesus was the embodiment of love. And so anyone who would take up their cross to follow Jesus must also take up love. Love shows the world that we belong to God (John 13:35). Love is the greatest magnet to draw unbelievers into the arms of God.

Therefore I challenge you. Be perfect. Become love. By doing so you will be following in His footsteps and become Christlike.

Chapter 13
HUMILITY AND SERVICE: THE WAY TO GREATNESS IN THE KINGDOM OF HEAVEN

Men aspire to be great by any means necessary. Their purpose and intention is to be recognized, to have others serve them, and to feel empowered. In this world, power and authority means "lording it over others" (Luke 22:35). They want to be in charge at any cost and tell others what to do without any care for their neighbor. This is the very attitude some of Jesus' disciples were beginning to take.

On more than one occasion, the disciples would argue amongst themselves about who would be the greatest in Jesus' kingdom. One time, while walking to Capernaum, they argued about this right after Jesus had spoken to them about His death (Mark 9:30-37). He then called a child over to Himself and placed the child on His lap to illustrate that greatness really comes by becoming childlike.

On another occasion, two of His disciples actually got their mother to ask Jesus to give her children the two highest positions in His kingdom (Matthew 20:20-28). She asked that one would sit on His left, and the other on His right. The other 10 disciples were extremely angry with this. I can imagine them saying, "Bro, for real? You got your mom to ask Jesus for the position? That's low." I'm pretty sure they were indignant, not because it was prideful or shrewd for them to have done such a thing, but because they wanted those positions themselves and probably didn't think about the idea of having their sweet momma's ask

Jesus first!

Yet, once again Jesus found Himself correcting this attitude in His disciples.

> ^{25} ...You know that the rulers of the Gentiles lord it over them, and *their* great men exercise authority over them. ^{26} It is not this way among you, but whoever wishes to become great among you shall be your servant, ^{27} and whoever wishes to be first among you shall be your slave; ^{28} just as the Son of Man did not come to be served, but to serve, and to give His life a ransom for many. (Matthew 20:25-28)

You would think that after correcting them a second time on this issue the disciples would've understood this point but they didn't.

The last time they had this argument it was actually in the upper room as they were celebrating the Passover. This is the night that Jesus would be betrayed, arrested and abandoned by His disciples. This time Jesus made Himself the example.

> ^{2} During supper, the devil having already put into the heart of Judas Iscariot, *the son* of Simon, to betray Him, ^{3} *Jesus*, knowing that the Father had given all things into His hands, and that He had come forth from God and was going back to God, ^{4} *got up from supper, and *laid aside His garments; and taking a towel, He girded Himself.

> ^{5} Then He *poured water into the basin, and

began to wash the disciples' feet and to wipe them with the towel with which He was girded... ¹² So when He had washed their feet, and taken His garments and reclined *at the table* again, He said to them, "Do you know what I have done to you? ¹³ You call Me Teacher and Lord; and you are right, for *so* I am. ¹⁴ If I then, the Lord and the Teacher, washed your feet, you also ought to wash one another's feet. ¹⁵ For I gave you an example that you also should do as I did to you. ¹⁶ Truly, truly, I say to you, a slave is not greater than his master, nor *is* one who is sent greater than the one who sent him. ¹⁷ If you know these things, you are blessed if you do them. (John 13:2-5, 12-17)

Jesus had to literally illustrate the attitude and actions His disciples should have toward one another. The disciples were focused on greatness, while Jesus wanted them to see that the path to greatness is through humility and service

Jesus is the very definition of humility. He humbled Himself by leaving His glory and power in heaven and taking on the limitations of man by becoming human (Philippians 2:6-8). He humbled Himself by being born in a manger (Luke 2:7). He humbled Himself by serving the multitudes and giving His life for the world (Mark 10:45). And as we saw in John 13, even on the night of His betrayal, Jesus humbled Himself like a slave and washed the feet of those who would betray, deny, and desert Him.

By his example, Jesus showed His disciples that you do not become great by taking advantage of others or by telling others what to do. You become great by becoming a slave, a servant of all. It is only when you humble yourself that God can exalt you. This might seem repulsive to some. It might seem illogical to consider the needs of others before your own and to see others as greater than yourself, but this is the way of Jesus, the way of the kingdom (Philippians 2:3-4).

If we want to be like Jesus then we are to find ways to help, serve, and give to others. In the kingdom of God true leaders are not those who are in charge but those who are willing to get on their hands and knees and "wash the feet" of their brothers and sisters. They are willing to be last in order that others may be first. They are willing to put their opinions, desires, and plans aside in order to help others fulfill God's calling for their lives. They are willing to tarnish their own reputation and image if it means demonstrating God's love.

How low can you go? How far are you willing to bend? How much are you willing to give up? Are there any ways that you could begin to serve right now? Maybe it's by taking out the trash at home, or helping your mother with her responsibilities around the house. Maybe you could volunteer at your church to clean the bathroom or help with the children's ministry or in the kitchen. Sometimes serving is as simple as holding a door open for someone who has their hands full. There is a kid's movie that had this for the moral, "see a need, fill a need." Are there any needs around you? How could you help?

The all-powerful, ever-present, all-knowing God was willing to give up everything if it meant having you. He didn't care that He was born in poverty. He didn't care if He was criticized for sitting and eating with "sinners" of the worst kind or that He carried out the work that belonged to the lowest of slaves. He was willing to not eat in order to reach one person (John 4). He was willing to sacrifice sleep and having "me time" in order to minister to the multitudes (Matthew 14). He was willing to be mistaken for a cursed, sinning imposter by dying on a cross between two thieves if it meant saving your life.

But listen to this! Because Jesus was willing to humble Himself to that extent, "God exalted Him to the highest place and gave Him a name that is above every name, that at the name of Jesus every knee should bow, in heaven and on earth and under the earth, and every tongue confess that Jesus Christ is Lord to the glory of God the Father" (Philippians 2:9-11). Exaltation is on the other side of humility. Greatness is on the other side of service. Glory is on the other side of sacrifice.

So, my question to you is, will you follow in His footsteps? Will you become Christlike? Will you humble yourself and serve others? Humility and service is the only way to greatness in the kingdom of Heaven.

Chapter 14
SUFFERING FOR RIGHTEOUSNESS

If there is any quality in the life of Jesus that is the most difficult to imitate but reaps the greatest reward, if endured – it's suffering for righteousness. As human beings, it is in our nature to avoid pain and seek comfort or pleasure. But the footprints of Jesus do not lead into comfort. His way is narrow and it is often laced with difficulty.

Though Christ came to bless, to save and to love, persecution met Him at every step. Not long after He was born men were sent to kill Him (Matthew 2:13). After His baptism at the age of 30, Satan came to tempt Him (Matthew 4:1-11). After one of the very first sermons He preached at Nazareth, his hometown, the people tried to throw Him over a cliff! (Luke 4:28-30). The religious leaders of His time hated Him and sought to kill him on various occasions (John 5:18; 7:1; 10:32-33). At the time of His greatest difficulty one friend betrayed Him, another denied Him, and the others just ran away. He was ultimately arrested, beaten, mocked, stripped of His clothes, spit on, whipped 39 times, and nailed hand and foot to a wooden cross!

Despite all of this, He never cursed or paid evil for evil; He never threatened anyone or committed sin (1 Peter 2:22-23). He remained true to His nature and calling. He loved, He forgave, and He even prayed for His enemies. Jesus endured all this to leave us with an example. "For you have been called for this purpose, since Christ also suffered for you, leaving you an example for you to follow in His steps" (1 Peter 2:21).

The Bible is very clear about what it means to follow Jesus. Consider carefully the path you're on to become like Him. We will be insulted, persecuted, hunted down aggressively, and falsely accused. We will be looked at as evil, close minded, archaic. The media will be manipulated against us, we will be lied about and cheated. We will be killed, hurt, and humiliated. This is even happening right now all over the world. And it will happen in your life if you are truly seeking to be like Him. "Indeed, all who desire to live godly in Christ Jesus will be persecuted" (2 Timothy 3:12).

Now, where will this persecution come from? Mostly from 5 different sources. The first is Satan. The Bible says, that Satan is a thief who comes to steal, kill and destroy (John 10:10). He will accuse us before God day and night (Revelation 12:10). He will oppose and hinder our attempts to preach the gospel (1 Thessalonians 2:18). Our battle is primarily against Satan and his demonic kingdom (Ephesians 6:12).

The second source of our persecution will be our own family and friends. Jesus said, "a man's enemies will be the members of his household" (Matthew 10:36). He also said, "21 Brother will betray brother to death, and a father *his* child; and children will rise up against parents and cause them to be put to death. 22 You will be hated by all because of My name, but it is the one who has endured to the end who will be saved" (10:21-22).

Third, we will be persecuted by the world. "Then they will deliver you to tribulation, and will kill you, and you will be hated by all nations because of My name" (Matthew 24:9).

18 If the world hates you, you know that it has hated Me before *it hated* you. 19 If you were of the world, the world would love its own; but because you are not of the world, but I chose you out of the world, because of this the world hates you. 20 Remember the word that I said to you, 'A slave is not greater than his master.' If they persecuted Me, they will also persecute you; if they kept My word, they will keep yours also.21 But all these things they will do to you for My name's sake, because they do not know the One who sent Me. (John 15:18-21)

Fourth, persecution will also come from other faiths and religions. "1 These things I have spoken to you so that you may be kept from stumbling. 2 They will make you outcasts from the synagogue, but an hour is coming for everyone who kills you to think that he is offering service to God. 3 These things they will do because they have not known the Father or Me" (John 16:1-3).

Lastly, and saddest of all, persecution shall come from within the church itself. Not everyone who claims to be of Christ, really is. There are false believers (2 Corinthians 11:26); false teachers, who use the gospel as a means for financial gain (2 Peter 2:1); false prophets, who are wolves in sheep's clothing (Matthew 7:15). Within every congregation there are tares among the wheat that have been planted by the evil one (Matthew 13:24-30). These people are "enemies of the cross" (Philippians 3:18).

But, what will be the cause of this persecution? Why would anyone want to hunt us down, or become hostile toward us because of our faith? It is primarily for two reasons. First, it will be because of our connection to Him. "But all these things they will do to you *for My name's sake*, because they do not know the One who sent Me" (John 15:21; emphasis mine). "Blessed are you when *people* insult you and persecute you, and falsely say all kinds of evil against you *because of Me*" (Matthew 5:11; emphasis mine).

Secondly, we will be persecuted for our connection to righteousness and stance against sin and injustice. As we live to obey God and stand against sin, our lives become like salt that is poured on open wounds; it becomes like a bright light that shines in darkness. We preserve what is good and expose what is evil. We have been called to preach a gospel that includes the word, "repent!"

To be a genuine disciple of Christ means that we will suffer persecution. Jesus said that anyone who is unwilling to pick up their cross, deny themselves and follow Him cannot be His disciple (Luke 14:27; 9:23).

But allow me to share the good news! We do not have to fear death or persecution (Matthew 10:28). There is a blessing pronounced over those who suffer for Jesus – "theirs is the kingdom of heaven!" (Matthew 5:10). You should rejoice because great will be your reward in heaven! (Matthew 5:12). Suffering for righteousness means that we get to identify with those heroes of old who have stood their ground before us (Matthew 5:12; Hebrews 11:32-38; 12:1-2). More than that, by sharing in the sufferings of Christ we will have deeper fellowship with Him (Philippians 3:10; 1 Peter 4:14, 16). We will also guarantee for ourselves a better and greater resurrection from the dead (Philippians 3:11; 2 Timothy 3:11-12; Hebrews 11:35; Revelation 20:6). The apostles understood this and were able to rejoice in times of great pain and persecution. "So they went on their way from the presence of the Council, rejoicing that they had been considered worthy to suffer shame for *His* name" (Acts 5:41).

We do not seek suffering nor desire it, but it is a reality every Christian will face. Knowing this doesn't make the pain and suffering any less real but it does give us hope that there is more in store for us on the other side of eternity. Even now, we can enjoy God's presence, love, peace and joy in the midst of persecution. He promises to be with us forever (Matthew 28:20).

The next great step in your journey to become like Him will lead you into suffering for righteousness. Suffering for righteousness is the way of Christ, and so suffering for righteousness is the way for His followers. This is one of the hallmarks of belonging to Christ and following Him. In order to become Christlike you must follow in His footsteps.

DISCIPLESHIP:
THE LIFE AND PRACTICE
OF MAKING DISCIPLES

Chapter 15
DISCIPLE-MAKING IS A LIFESTYLE

Jesus said that His followers were to go into all the world, preach the gospel and make disciples of all nations (Matthew 28:19; Mark 16:15). The first thing I want you to know about these words is that they are not a suggestion, they are a command from our King. We are literally to "go," "preach," "make disciples," and "teach them" which involves action, moving, intentionally and deliberately taking steps to draw others to Christ and help them become more like Him.

The second thing I want you to know about these words is that they are not for elite Christians, perfect people, or ministers. Jesus expects *every* follower of His to be involved in the process of making disciples. This means you. This means me. This means the recent convert and even the most experienced disciple. We are all called to find ways to share the good news with others, and then form intentional relationships for the purpose of helping one another grow in the character, knowledge and power of Jesus Christ.

For too long we have relegated the work of making disciples to the pastor or leaders of the church. We have been overly dependent on using ministries, activities and programs to make disciples. The problem with this, according to Greg Ogden, in his book *Transforming Discipleship*, is first, "Programs tend to be information – or knowledge based."[18] Some people assume that the more information one has the better disciple one will make.

---

[18] Greg Ogden, *Transforming Discipleship* (Downers Grove, Illinois: Intervarsity Press, 2003), 43.

Churches can sometimes assume that, "right knowledge will produce right living."[19] If this were true, Christians in the West, with all their Bibles, conferences, sermons, classes, books, institutes and universities should be the most holy and on-fire Christians the world has ever seen. Sadly, in this moment in time, the opposite can be said.

Second, he says, "Programs are the one preparing for the many."[20] The problem with this is that only a few do the hard work of preparation and investment while others usually sit back and remain receivers. Third, Ogden relates, "Programs are characterized by regimentation or synchronization."[21] The problem with this is that "Every individual is unique and different. Making disciples requires a customized approached."[22] Lastly, "Programs generally have low personal accountability."[23] Many times programs focus more on people finishing a curriculum than actually practicing and exercising what they have learned.

Now, let me say this; Programs, services, activities, classes or ministries are not bad as long as they serve, and do not replace the relational dynamic that is supposed to be involved in making disciples. Making disciples involves more than providing information; it is more than a curriculum. It involves relationships, life investment, love, and accountability.

Greg Ogden defines discipleship as a "process that takes place within accountable relationships over a period of time for the purpose of bringing believers into spiritual

---

[19] Ibid, 43.
[20] Ibid, 44.
[21] Ibid, 45.
[22] Ibid, 45.
[23] Ibid, 45.

maturity in Christ."[24] In other words, for us to make disciples we must be in relationship with other people. But these relationships must have a goal, a purpose. It is not just to fellowship and hang out. That purpose or goal must be to help one another reach "spiritual maturity in Christ."

Another facet in Ogden's definition of discipleship is accountability. This means a willingness to be open about our failures and sins. This means being willing to listen to correction and be challenged to conform our lives to Jesus and His words. Accountability implies trust, transparency, honesty, love, encouragement and comfort. Ogden recommends that there be even a contract stating the purpose and expectations of this relationship, so that everyone is accountable and responsible for their behavior and lifestyle.

Now, in order to accomplish this, we must be willing to spend time with those we are discipling. Discipleship is a process. We must be willing to sacrifice, or better said, *invest* our time in other people. Making disciples is not about seeing each other in church once a week, but about walking side by side; "doing life together." We must be willing to meet with these people outside of a church service. We should care for one another, carry one another's burdens, and talk to and pray for one another.

It is important that you see yourself as a disciple who will make disciples. And making disciples is not about completing a program or finishing a curriculum. Discipleship is a lifestyle. Making disciples should be your lifestyle. Until you feel ready to lead others, submit yourself to a leader or group of people that can keep you

---

[24] Ibid, 54.

accountable and will be willing to walk with you until you are mature or strong enough to lead and disciple others. Great followers make great leaders. But don't stay a follower. Make disciple-making a lifestyle. For it is a part of Jesus' Great Commission not great suggestion.

Chapter 16
DISCIPLESHIP WITHIN A COMMUNITY

It has become a fad in many places for people to call themselves Christians and yet not want to be a part of any local church. These people say things like, "I don't have to go to Church to believe in God" or "I can worship God right from my house." Many times those who speak this way have either been hurt by someone in a church or have rebellious tendencies. Others are looking for "the perfect" place to worship.

I want to say this clearly, you cannot grow into a fully mature Christian without the Church. It is important that if you or anyone that you are discipling want to mature and grow in this walk with Christ, you must be a part of a local body of believers. Terry Wardle, in his book *Outrageous Love, Transforming Power*, says,

> Christians who are at all concerned about becoming like Jesus, must know this: there are some aspects of spiritual maturity that can only be developed within a caring Christian community.....A person who claims to be a follower of Christ is by nature a person committed to community. Granted, that commitment may need to be developed. But Christianity is all about a people united together under the Lordship of Jesus Christ.[25]

---

[25] Terry Wardle, *Outrageous Love, Transforming Power* (Siloam Springs, Arkansas: Leafwood Publishers, 2004), 62 and 63.

In other words if we want Christ, we have to accept all of Him including His family. It is only within the context of His family and community that we will truly ever grow and mature as disciples.

Living as "lonely or solitary" Christians is the reason why many people do not last in this walk. And those who do last usually don't mature in many areas of their Christian walk, especially when it comes to relationships. Forming a discipline of coming together or congregating is necessary. As someone once told me "predators like to go after prey that have been separated from their flock."

What is the Church?

The word we use for "church" comes from the Greek word "ekklesia," which literally refers to an assembly of people.[26] In the New Testament, the word "church" can be seen, primarily, in two different ways:

1. All believers in Christ at all times and places (catholic[27] or universal church)

2. Specific group of believers together at a certain location (local church or congregation)

So this means that when we speak of the "Church" we are not referring to a building, or four walls, or a specific denomination. But we are speaking about a living organism, a body of believers who have a sole purpose and

---

[26] In ancient times this was usually the coming together of the citizens in a city.

[27] By "Catholic" I do not mean the denomination known as the Roman Catholic Church but *catholic* as in "universal," which is what it means.

goal to be like their master. Millard Erickson makes a sharp observation of the Church when he says, "the church is the continuation of the Lord's presence and ministry in the world."[28]

The Need to Congregate in a Local Church

At conversion you were made a part of the universal body of Christ, but you must also seek a local church where you can congregate with other believers. We are to form a discipline for gathering as a Church in the same fashion we discipline ourselves to pray, read, fast, worship, give, and evangelize. When we congregate we are:

1. Obeying the Bible

Hebrews 10:25 says, "not forsaking our own assembling together, as is the habit of some, but encouraging *one another*; and all the more as you see the day drawing near." Observe from this verse, first of all, that we should not forsake our "assembling together." This is not referring to small, informal fellowship gatherings but to the official coming together as a church.

Second, that there are many who, even in those days, are in "the habit" of doing so. A habit is a regular practice. It is something acquired by repetition. It is a norm not an exception. There will be days that you might not be able to go to church, but you should not let that turn into a habit. If you allow this to become repetitive sometimes habits become second nature, they become so normal to us that we

---

[28] Millard Erickson, *Introducing Christian Doctrine* (Grand Rapids, Michigan: Baker Academic, 2001), 345.

don't even notice when we're doing it. There are some believers who miss church habitually and it's like nothing to them to miss a Sunday service here, a Bible class there, a prayer meeting over here, and a small group session over there.

Third, observe that we should assemble "all the more." As "the day" for Jesus' return draws closer we should congregate more, not less. We have become so infatuated with this world and with our earthly pleasures that we don't want more church, we want less. We want our Sunday services to run an hour or two and no more. Many churches don't even have prayer meetings anymore during the week. It's no wonder that we don't have revival. The Holy Spirit will not submit to our time and convenience. We must submit to His.

So as we can see from this verse, it is wrong to not congregate or be a part of a local church. Of course there are exceptions, which I am not going to get into now, but as a norm every believer needs to congregate regularly at a local church.

2. Blessing and being blessed

1 Corinthians 12:27 says, "Now you are Christ's body, and individually members of it." Each part of the human body is necessary and important. Every part has a function and a purpose. When any of the body parts are missing or hurting, the whole body suffers. In the same way, every believer is a part of the body of Jesus. Each person, including you or the person you are discipling, has a function, a purpose, a specific role to fulfill. Whenever

you are not fulfilling your part the whole body suffers. Whenever you are fulfilling your purpose the whole body is built up. I don't care how small or insignificant you feel or see yourself. You make a difference!

Not only can you be a blessing to others, but others can be a blessing to you. In the same way your gifts, talents, and service helps others, theirs will do the same for you. It is by serving one another that we grow. In fact, God has given certain gifts or ministries to the church "[12] for the equipping of the saints for the work of service, to the building up of the body of Christ; [13] until we all attain to the unity of the faith, and of the knowledge of the Son of God, to a mature man, to the measure of the stature which belongs to the fullness of Christ" (Ephesians 4:12-13).

Even the smallest things we do for each other matter. We don't have to have positions of leadership to bless others or be blessed. I could not tell you the countless times when someone's hug, smile, or encouraging word has lifted my spirit and inspired me to do greater things for God. This book is an example of that! I have also been able to help others through my giving, teaching, praying, or serving. Everything we do to and for one another drives us closer to being like Jesus (Hebrews 10:24).

3. *Telling the world Jesus is real!*

John 17:21 says, "that they may all be one; even as You, Father, *are* in Me and I in You, that they also may be in Us, so that the world may believe that You sent Me." Our unity shouts to the world, "Jesus is real and He is awesome!" I mean, what else could make enemies forgive and love each other? What else could bring people from different backgrounds, ages, genders, races and colors together? Is it not His blood? Is it not His Spirit? Is it not the common salvation that we share?

When we congregate we are telling the world "I truly believe in Christ, He makes a difference, not only in what I believe, but how I live!" The opposite is also true. When we don't congregate, when we don't care to gather with other believers we are saying, "This is just something religious for me. Christ really doesn't make a difference. He isn't that important to me." And of course this is not just about coming together religiously, but coming together in love and unity that preaches to the world that Jesus is truly sent by God.

4. Being Sharpened

Proverbs 27:17 says, as "Iron sharpens iron, So one man sharpens another." As we come into contact with other believers we will need to deal with different characters, personalities, and situations that will help test us and mold us. I've heard many people say, "The church is like a hospital." This means that not everyone in the church is at the same level of maturity spiritually or emotionally. This can sometimes cause conflict or friction. How we handle or respond to these situations will help us develop and put into practice the fruit of the Spirit. Especially the fruits of love, patience, meekness and self-control.

But this is not the only way we are sharpened. As we sit under the teaching of the Word of God, we will be instructed, challenged, rebuked and corrected in order to be trained to live righteously and work for the kingdom of God (2 Timothy 3:16-17). We will also learn how to live in submission to authority, as we obey and follow the teachings and examples of the elders and leaders of the church. This will help to mold the areas of humility and faithfulness in our lives.

Being sharpened isn't always fun or exciting. But it is always productive and edifying if we allow ourselves to be molded.

Finding a Healthy Church

There isn't a perfect church anywhere in the world. But there are healthy, thriving churches. As we have already mentioned, if you or the person you are discipling are going to grow and mature it's important to find a place that you can call your "home" church. This should be the place where you can attend regularly and learn to be a better disciple of Christ.

But how do you find a healthy church or a church that is right for you? This is something that I have been asked on many occasions. Let me share some general qualities that a healthy church should have which would make it ideal for you to take root there. This is not an exhaustive list, but it should definitely point you in the right direction.

1. A healthy church is an orthodox church

"Orthodox" is made up of two Greek words, "ortho" and "doxa." *Ortho* can mean straight or right, and *doxa* can mean opinion. When used in reference to Christianity "orthodox" or "orthodoxy" is referring to right, correct, or accepted teachings or beliefs. This means that any church you attend should hold or believe in the right, correct or accepted teachings of the Christian faith. Of course, every church will differ on certain topics, but the main, core doctrines and beliefs of that church should be orthodox. Christians can disagree on secondary issues,[29] but they should agree on the primary issues.

The primary issues that Christians agree on that make a church orthodox have to do with who God is and the things He has done and will do. These core beliefs are summarized in what is known as the Apostles Creed.[30] The creed says the following:

> ***I believe in God the Father, Almighty,***
> ***Maker of heaven and earth;***
> ***And in Jesus Christ, his only begotten Son,***
> ***our Lord;***
> ***Who was conceived by the Holy Ghost,***
> ***born of the Virgin Mary;***
> ***Suffered under Pontius Pilate; was***
> ***crucified, dead and buried;***
> ***He descended into hades;***
> ***The third day he rose again from the dead;***
> ***He ascended into heaven, and sits at the***
> ***right hand of God the Father Almighty;***

---

[29] Secondary issues are things like, does the rapture happen before, in the middle, or after the tribulation? what is the baptism of the Holy Spirit and what is the evidence that it has occurred?

[30] It is named the Apostles Creed not because the apostles created or wrote it, but because it summarized the doctrines that they taught and passed down to the next generation of believers.

From thence he shall come to judge the
quick and the dead;
I believe in the Holy Ghost;
I believe in the holy catholic[31] church;
the communion of saints;
The forgiveness of sins;
The resurrection of the body;
And the life everlasting. Amen.

A church that does not hold to these beliefs would not be considered orthodox. It does not hold to the core, traditional values of the Christian faith and should therefore be avoided.

2. A healthy church is a biblical church

A biblical church is a church that, first and foremost, believes that the Bible is the inspired, inerrant, and authoritative Word of God. By *inspired* I mean that the Bible comes from God. That even though it was written by men, the Holy Spirit led each of these men to write what they wrote.[32] By *inerrant* I mean that because the Bible is ultimately from God it contains no errors. It is perfect and true without any faults. And if the Bible comes from God and has no errors or mistakes then it must be *authoritative*. By authoritative I mean that everything we do and believe should be in line with what the Bible says. We are to measure everything by the word of God. My life should be

---

[31] Notice this is "catholic" with a lowercase "c" not a capital "C." When it's lowercase it means universal, when it's uppercase it is referring to the Roman Catholic Church.
[32] See 2 Timothy 3:16-17 and 2 Peter 1:19-21.

in submission to God's Word.

Secondly, a biblical church is a church that preaches the Bible. It literally teaches and proclaims the truths found in the Scriptures without twisting, perverting, or misinterpreting it to the best of one's ability. In our days, there are many people who preach tradition and opinions instead of the Word of God. Tradition is important and so are our opinions, but we must submit any tradition, opinion, vision, or experience to the Word.

3. A healthy church is a Spirit empowered and Spirit led church

Although this might sound mean, religious, or close minded, I am convinced that a church that leaves no room for the Holy Spirit to lead and empower believers is a dead church. I am aware of the many branches of Christianity and denominations who each have their own forms of liturgy (styles of worship and order in a service). But many times our rigid structures and our commitment to traditional worship for the sake of maintaining "order" has both quenched and grieved the Spirit of God.

In the West we have elevated reason and intellect to such a level that we reject the spontaneous moving of God's Spirit. Anything that looks like passion, enthusiasm, or too emotional has become dangerous and threatening. I call this man centered religion. I call this man controlled religion.

But let me tell you, God cannot be put in a box. He cannot be controlled nor can He be manipulated. From its very inception the church has been a body of believers that is empowered by the Spirit of God and led by this same

112

Spirit. He touches people today. He speaks to people today. This hasn't stopped. And any church that prohibits His freedom to move and minister as He chooses is an unhealthy church.[33]

4. A healthy church is a loving church

Paul said,

> [1] If I speak with the tongues of men and of angels, but do not have love, I have become a noisy gong or a clanging cymbal. [2] If I have *the gift of* prophecy, and know all mysteries and all knowledge; and if I have all faith, so as to remove mountains, but do not have love, I am nothing. [3] And if I give all my possessions to feed *the poor*, and if I surrender my body to be burned, but do not have love, it profits me nothing. (1 Corinthians 13:1-3)

What this means is even if a church is greatly used of God in supernatural ways, but it has no love, it is an unhealthy church. You want to be somewhere where the brothers and sisters love each other, care for one another and are not attacking or gossiping about one another, rather they are known for serving and encouraging one another.

---

[33] By this I am not suggesting that churches with traditional styles of worship or structured liturgy cannot be Spirit empowered or led. I am also not suggesting that only Pentecostal or charismatic churches are Spirit empowered or led. In fact, in both cases men can possiblly be controlling and manipulating people's emotions or will. What I am saying is that any church that doesn't give freedom to the Holy Spirit to empower, touch, guide, or lead the people as He desires is an abnormal church according to the Bible.

5. A healthy church is a praying church

It is possible for a church to be extremely organized, have many programs, be involved with the community and yet be a dry church. This point connects with point three, but I want to emphasize the need for every church to be a church of prayer. The Scriptures even mention that God's house should be a house of prayer (Isaiah 56:7; Matthew 21:13). Every church should believe in the power of prayer and practice it. A healthy church will be a church that prays to seek God's direction and prays to see God intervene in the daily affairs of its members and community.

When I speak of a praying church, I am not referring to one minute dry prayers tacked on to a program or service. I mean that time is taken before a service, during a service, or after a service for prayer. Or possibly a whole segment of time is separated during the week for prayer. Besides what is done congregationally, a praying church will encourage its members to pray in secret. A praying pulpit begets a praying pew.

6. A healthy church is an evangelizing church

It's very simple, a church that does not evangelize will die. Jesus told us to go into all the world and preach the gospel and make disciples of all the nations. A church that does not evangelize is a church that does not care about the Great Commission. A church that does not evangelize is a church that does not care about souls. A church that does not evangelize will eventually begin to dwindle in number and close down. For a church to remain healthy it must continually infuse its body with new life which comes greatly through the winning of souls. When a church stops reaching out to unbelievers it loses its passion, it loses its fire, it loses its vision and purpose and eventually will lose its very soul.

Get Involved

If you want to grow as a disciple or help someone else grow in Christlikeness, you must find a healthy local church. You do this by asking questions and observing to see if the church is orthodox, biblical, Spirit-empowered and Spirit-led, loving, praying, and evangelizing.

You don't have to make a commitment to become a member immediately, but once you have prayed and have peace about your decision you should seek to get involved in the life of the church. It will do you no good to be a spectator and watch from the outside. As has been said by many, if you stand in a garage it will not make you a car. In the same way, just because you attend services at a church it will not make you more like Christ. You must participate, you must get your hands dirty, connect with people, serve in any way you can. If you are faithful in the small things, God will give you grace and open up more opportunities to grow and help others.

It's ok if the church isn't perfect. It's ok if the church has differences or doesn't provide everything you're seeking. You might not agree with every decision or the way it's organized. But if it has those six main qualities I have mentioned it is possibly a healthy place for you to grow or disciple others. Don't become a church hopper. Don't remain a religious spectator. Get involved, integrate yourself, and God will lead you and help you become a blessing to others.

Chapter 17
THE POWER OF SMALL GROUPS

We live in a day of superstars, big macs, and mega churches. We want everything supersized. In our minds, the bigger the better; and the more we have the happier we are. Yet in the kingdom, greatness comes from humility and abundant fruit from a mustard seed. When it comes to discipleship less is more.

When Jesus decided to establish His kingdom He did not spend the majority of His time discipling the multitudes. Instead, He invested three and a half years of His life in 12 men. We know them as the twelve apostles. He taught the multitudes in parables yet shared the secrets of the kingdom with the 12. He ministered and healed the crowds, yet He empowered the 12 with the same authority He exercised.

Although Jesus wanted to save a world of lost people, He invested His life in a small group of men who would in turn reach the world. By investing in a few, He multiplied His own life, ministry, teachings, and power in the men He discipled. Jesus' strategy of ministry teaches us about the value and power of small groups.

Advantages of Small Groups

There is nothing wrong with wanting a church or a ministry to grow, or for multitudes to turn to Christ. The problem comes when the multitudes are seen as numbers instead of individuals who need to grow in their relationship with Jesus. And for growth in Christ to happen there are essential ingredients that must exist. These ingredients or qualities are difficult to find when a person is just a number amongst the crowd. These ingredients include: personalized instruction, intimate relationships, and discipline and accountability.

1. Personalized instruction

Henry Ford, the founder of the Ford car company, created a standard car that was economical for people of different financial classes. He did this by building cars through an assembly line. Every car would go through the same process and get the same parts. This allowed for many cars to be produced at a low cost.

Many times we treat disciple making like an assembly line. We have everyone, regardless of age, gender, educational background, or experience, go through the same classes and programs and believe that at the end it should create a standard Christian. It's low cost and can work on a great number of people at once. Yet in the end, we notice that the product (disciple) doesn't always come out with high quality.

Maybe we should stop treating the Great Commission like an assembly line and more like a small garden where every flower or tree is tended to personally. We can tailor our ministry to fit the needs and backgrounds of each individual. This is something that can happen in a small group.

With less people, we can instruct, teach, counsel and train each person on a one on one level. Any teacher will tell you that it is easier to teach a class of 10 than a class of

40. The teaching becomes more personal. The student can ask more questions, the teacher can invest more time. This leads me to the second advantage of a small group.

2. Intimate relationships

Teaching isn't the only ingredient needed to help someone mature in their walk with Christ. People need friendship. They need to know that they matter and that someone cares enough to invest time in them. They need a listening ear and a shoulder to cry on when things are difficult. They need someone they can just hang out with and have fun. They need wise counsel and someone who is willing to take time out of their schedule just to be with them.

Do you realize that Jesus literally ate, slept, talked, laughed, counseled, and lived with His 12 disciples, every day and every night for three and a half years? Even among that small group there were three whom He even allowed into His innermost circle. Peter, James and John were able to see Jesus Transfigured (Matthew 17, Mark 9, Luke 9), raise a girl from the dead (Mark 5), and agonize in prayer in the Garden of Gethsemane (Matthew 26, Mark 14, Luke 22).

I am not saying that you should abandon everyone and everything and live with someone you are discipling 24 hours a day and seven days a week. What I am saying is growth in Christ comes through people investing their lives in one another and creating intimate relationships. This is difficult to do in large groups.

3. Discipline and accountability

A discipleship relationship within a small group is not a friendship that has no goals. These relationships are formed around the goal of growing in Christlikeness. This means there should be rules, structure, and discipline. Each person should live in submission to Christ and one another. Ephesians 5:21 says, "be subject to one another in the fear of Christ." In other words, those within a small group should be held accountable for how they live and the choices they make.

As Christians we are called to live holy lives in obedience to the Lord Jesus Christ. When someone is practicing sin, it is appropriate and loving to confront, correct, and counsel such a person. Of course, this should be done with gentleness and respect, remembering that we want to treat others the way we would like to be treated (Matthew 7:12).

Although, we shall all give an account to God individually for our lives, in this life we are our brother's keeper (Genesis 4:9). We should carry one another's burdens. "[1] Brethren, even if anyone is caught in any trespass, you who are spiritual, restore such a one in a spirit of gentleness; *each one* looking to yourself, so that you too will not be tempted. [2] Bear one another's burdens, and thereby fulfill the law of Christ" (Galatians 6:1-2).

Personalized instruction, intimate relationships, and discipline and accountability is very difficult to experience or do with a large group of people. But within a small group, healthy discipleship can take place and people can grow in spiritual maturity.

Our Small Group Structure

For as long as I can remember, I have had a desire to see my church incorporate small groups into its structure. I have benefited personally from relationships that included these ingredients, and believed that it would be a blessing to more people if the church got involved as a whole.

I read many books on the subject[34] and each one helped contribute to the small group structure I now use at my church. The general structure of our small groups is based on John Wesley's class meeting. John Wesley is considered an expert in the field of small groups. The essence of his class meetings had to do with engaging the heart. Each person in the small group would answer questions about their walk with God. For example, "how does your soul prosper?" In other words, how is your life with God?

These questions helped each person give an account of how they were living. Based on their answers they would receive encouragement, support, prayer or correction. It allowed the leaders to minister to the hearts of each Christian and not just their minds.

In our church, the people are divided into groups of no more than 10 or 12. These groups can meet in different homes or the church for a designated period of time. Each

---

[34] Although there are many books and materials to instruct people on the topic of small groups I want to recommend the following: *The Class Meeting* by Kevin M. Watson; *Transforming Discipleship* by Greg Ogden; *8 Habits of Effective Small Group Leaders* by Dave Earley; *The Complete Book of Discipleship* by Bill Hull; and *Creating Community* by Andy Stanley and Bill Willits.

group is given a contract that stipulates the rules and expectations of the group and each member. Although each week, the activities that are done in the group may vary, the highlight of the groups are the times when they get to share their hearts and then pray and minister to one another.

By the grace of God, these groups have become such a blessing. People have been touched and ministered to greatly. There are people that I considered to be enemies or a danger to my ministry and to the church, but after implementing this particular small group method they have become some of my greatest supporters and workers at the church. The transformation and maturity that has taken place in many of the members has been enormous.

Creating a Small Group Structure for You

If you want to create a small group culture in your church or participate in one, the first thing I would recommend you do is get informed. You cannot do something that you have no knowledge of. Read books, attend conferences, and speak to others who have experience with small groups. Find out the pros and cons, the strengths and weakness, the blessings and difficulties, and even the different types of small groups.

Second, I would say to speak to your pastor or leaders about this topic. Small groups should be a blessing. You should not implement anything that might go against your pastor, or the vision of your church. If they give you the green light then proceed to the next step. If they say no, do not rebel or speak against your leaders. Pray, continue growing personally, and wait for a better opportunity. Some churches have had negative experiences with small groups and can be a little resistant to the idea. But if you come humbly, with sufficient information, and lots of prayer God can touch their hearts.

Third, you should pray for God to help you choose what kind of small group to develop and what people you want to connect with. It's important to be clear about the rules and expectations of the group when you ask anyone to become a part of it. Additionally, since these people will be connecting with you and with one other for an extended period of time, it's important that God has been involved in the process from beginning to end.

Don't be afraid of the dynamics of forming these groups. No matter how informed or experienced you are, it is possible that difficulties can arise. But you can minimize and learn ways to handle these problems in a healthy way. If your intention and the desire of those in your small group is to mature spiritually and become more like Jesus, God will help you navigate through the uncertainties.

Chapter 18
MAKE DISCIPLES OF ALL NATIONS

In the Bible, there are many symbols that are used to describe believers. Christians are described as members of the body of Christ (1 Corinthians 12:27), living stones (1 Peter 2:5), temples of the Holy Spirit (1 Corinthians 6:19), branches of the True vine (John 15:5), and sheep of the Good Shepherd (John 10). But there are two symbols that impact greatly how we can fulfill the Great Commission and disciple the nations. Those are the symbols of salt and light.

We are the Salt of the Earth and Light of the World

In Matthew 5:13-16, believers are described as the "salt of the earth" and the "light of the world." Each of these two symbols represent the different ways we influence the world for Christ. Together, these two elements will describe how we are to impact our world.

Salt of the earth

In the days of Jesus, salt was used in different ways. One of the ways salt was used was as a condiment which is a substance that is used to add flavor to food. But, salt was also used as a preservative. Refrigerators weren't invented until the 19th Century. So when the people in Jesus' time wanted to preserve their meat, like fish or lamb, they would use salt. The properties in salt helped to keep the meat from decaying.

And so when Jesus says we are salt He is saying that we are a people that give real flavor and life to this world,

125

but even more than that – we keep this world from decaying, from destroying itself, from dying. Without salt, the meat in Jesus' day would decay and rot. In the same way, without the Church, without Christians, without the people of God this world would decay and rot all by itself.

Notice that wherever genuine Christians are, they influence for good. They are the salt in their homes. They make peace between family members that are at enmity with each other. They are salt in their communities. They share the message of salvation and the love of Christ with people who are lost in darkness and find themselves without any hope. They are salt in their nations. They stand against, protest and vote against injustice. They are the salt of the world. They preach and pray and intercede for the lost.

Think about it, where would we be if it wasn't for the Christian and Spokesperson, William Wilberforce, who stood up against the most powerful nation and empire at that time and fought against slavery? Or where would this nation be if it wasn't for the Christian and Pastor, Martin Luther King? We would still be living in the bitterness of hatred and racism.

Christians are the salt of the earth. As long as Christians are true, genuine, obedient, holy, loving, different, distinct and courageous they keep this world from death, decay and darkness.

Light of the world

Christians are not only the salt of the earth, they are the light of the world. Jesus identifies us as light, and by

126

doing so He is identifying the world as darkness. That means we, as believers, are the light in the middle of the darkness. And as light our influence in this world penetrates, promotes and illuminates.

While Jesus was on this earth, He said He was the light of the world. But He knew He was going to leave one day, and as the Church, as His body, we are to carry His title and continue the responsibility of being light in this world full of darkness.

Now what is the purpose of light? By looking at how natural light works, we will know how we are to work as light. The purpose of light is to *expose* and to *illuminate*. First, it is the responsibility of the light to expose, disperse and remove darkness. Second, it is the responsibility of the light to illuminate, to reveal what couldn't be seen and to provide guidance to where someone needs to go.

It is also important to know something else about the light before we can begin to see clearly how this applies to us. The Bible uses light as a symbol or metaphor of two things: the Word of God, "Your word is a lamp to my feet, a light to my path" (Psalm 119:105); and good works "Let your light shine before men in such a way that they may see your good works, and glorify your Father who is in heaven" (Matthew 5:16).

So if we put everything we know about light together, naturally and biblically, we can see that as light we expose darkness and illuminate the way for the world to know God and to know His will through the preaching of the Word of God and by our good works. In other words, with the Word of God, our example, our way of living, and our good works we expose the darkness, evil, and sin in this world; we show the world that the path they're on leads to death, and its way of living, thinking, and speaking are wrong. Then we show them a better way.

Salt needs to be in the midst of what's decaying in order to preserve. Light needs to be in the middle of darkness in order to illumine the way and expose what's in the dark. But when Christians don't go into the world and don't disciple nations we become like worthless and damaging salt, or like a good for nothing lamp because it's being covered.

Climbing the Seven Mountains

Did you know that serving within a church isn't the only way to serve God and influence people for Christ? If we want to be salt and light in a way that not only impacts individuals who come to our services but whole nations or groups of people outside our churches, we should seek to be involved in the places that reach the most amount of persons.

Lance Wallnau, in *Invading Babylon: The 7 Mountain Mandate*, speaks about 7 areas of society that shape culture and greatly influences a nation. He calls these seven areas, seven mountains. Of these mountains he says,

> Each of the seven mountains represents an individual sphere of influence that shapes the way people think. These mountains are crowned with high places that modern-day kings occupy as ideological strongholds.

These strongholds are, in reality, houses built out of thoughts. These thought structures are fortified with spiritual reinforcement that shapes the culture and establishes the spiritual climate of each nation. I sensed the Lord telling me, "He who can take these mountains can take the harvest of nations."[35]

What this means is that if believers will occupy these seven mountains, they will have the greatest influence over society as a whole. Is it possible the world has gained so much power and influence over our nation because Christians have abandoned these mountains and handed it over to the enemy?

It is interesting to note, that Bill Johnson also says of these mountains that Christians should not see them as secular. He says, "As the people of God move into these realms of society to show forth the benefits and values of the Kingdom, His government expands."[36] Again he says,

There is no such thing as secular employment for the believer. Once we are born again, everything about us is redeemed for Kingdom purposes. It is all spiritual. It is either a legitimate Kingdom expression, or we shouldn't be involved at all.

Every believer is in full-time ministry – only a few have pulpits in sanctuaries. The rest

---

[35] Lance Wallnau and Bill Johnson, *Invading Babylon: The 7 Mountain Mandate* (Shippensburg, PA: Destiny Image Publishers, 2013), 54.
[36] Ibid, 23.

have their pulpit in their areas of expertise and favor in the world system.[37]

Christians should see all of what they do as an opportunity to spread the gospel and bring glory to God.

Now, what are these seven mountains, these 7 areas of influence that can greatly help shape and transform culture or a nation? The seven mountains are:

1. The Church
2. Home (Family)
3. Education
4. Government and Politics
5. Media (television, radio, newspaper, Internet)
6. Arts, Entertainment, sports
7. Business (Commerce, science, and technology)

As you read this list, I would like for you to ask yourself some questions. Are homes so broken because the Church isn't as involved as it should be? Is our education system so flawed because the Church isn't as involved as it should be? Is our government and the politics so corrupt because the Church isn't as involved as it should be? Is the media, our television programs, and the internet so degrading because the Church isn't as involved as it should be? Are our sports, entertainment, music, and art so poisoning because the Church isn't as involved as it should be? Are businesses, science, and technology becoming so harmful to society because the Church isn't as involved as it should be?

---

[37] Ibid, 23-24

What difference would it make if true, Bible believing, Holy Spirit filled Christians were the greatest influencers in these areas? What difference would we make for the gospel if, instead of abandoning our place in these areas, we actually became the leaders? How could we transform the minds of the younger generations if we were salt and light in all of these areas?

I am not advocating that we should take these mountains by force nor that we convert the world by the sword, nor that we try and create a theocracy here on the earth. No. Jesus Christ will come soon and He will establish His kingdom on the earth and will rule righteously and perfectly. What I am trying to encourage us to do is be at the front of the battle in these areas so that we can make the greatest impact and change the destinies of not only individuals, but nations for the generations to come.

I encourage you to make more money so that you can fund the kingdom. I encourage you to aspire for higher positions in all these areas so that you can have more influence and help more people. I encourage you not to abandon those places where things seem the darkest in order to hide in the church amongst other believers. Do not be overcome by the world, but overcome it by your faith. By doing this you will contribute to fulfilling the Great Commission and making disciples of all nations.

Chapter 19
DISCIPLE YOUR FAMILY

Family is the foundational unit for any society. If the family is healthy, society will be healthy. If the family is unhealthy, so will the society be. The ideal family that serves as a strong basis for a healthy society is a family under the Lordship of Jesus; a family where everyone knows their roles and fulfills them.

Family According to Scripture

Presently, there is so much confusion. There are no longer males and females, but many different genders. There is no true solid definition as to what a family is. Recently, the Supreme Court has even redefined marriage. But the Bible is very clear about what a family is.

The most basic unit of any family is the union, in life-long marriage, between one man and one female. Matthew 19:4-6 says,

> [4] ...Have you not read that He who created *them* from the beginning made them male and female, [5] and said, "For this reason a man shall leave his father and mother and be joined to his wife, and the two shall become one flesh"? [6] So they are no longer two, but one flesh. What therefore God has joined together, let no man separate.

Family begins with one man, one male, one husband uniting to one woman, one female, and one wife. Although this seems obvious to some, obviously this is not the view of society now a days.

If a husband and wife choose to procreate then the fruit of their love produces children. This in turn changes the role of the man to husband/father and the woman to wife/mother. Neither party sacrifices one role for the other. They both take on additional responsibilities and privileges with the change in parenthood. In other words, the man still has the responsibility to love his wife and at the same time care for his children, and vice versa with the woman.

The Roles of Each Member

Now if we look at the roles of each member of the family we can see that the man has the responsibility of being the head of the home. He is the "priest," the leader, the provider, the instructor, the vision caster. The wife is the "help mate" (Genesis 2:18), the caretaker of the home, and a virtuous woman who is able to carry on business outside the home for the sake of her family. The children are to be trained up in the way they should go. They are accountable to their parents while they are still under their authority. Paul instructs each member of the family as follows,

> [18] Wives, be subject to your husbands, as is fitting in the Lord. [19] Husbands, love your wives and do not be embittered against them. [20] Children, be obedient to your parents in all things, for this is well-pleasing to the Lord. [21] Fathers, do not exasperate your children, so that they will not lose heart. (Colossians 3:18-20)

Fathers Are to Teach Their Children

In a parallel passage to Colossians 3, Paul gives similar instructions to the family. When it comes to children he adds, "Fathers, do not provoke your children to anger, but bring them up in the discipline and instruction of the Lord" (Ephesians 6:4). Notice there are two primary responsibilities that is laid upon the Father in a home in this verse. They are to bring up their children in the "*discipline* and *instruction* of the Lord*.*" The discipline and instruction of the Lord is a reference both to teaching and a way of living. This includes correction, rebuke, and admonishment.

In other words, Fathers are to help train their children in maintaining a lifestyle that is rooted in Christ and is to teach them the doctrines and commandments of the Lord. That responsibility is not primarily to be upon the pastor, Sunday school teacher, nor any leader within the church. The main person responsible for training and teaching the child is the father. Of course the mother should be just as involved in this process. The point I am trying to make is that true discipleship begins at home through the parents, not at church through any leaders.

We see this very instruction in the Old Testament. "⁶ These words, which I am commanding you today, shall be on your heart. ⁷ You shall teach them diligently to your sons and shall talk of them when you sit in your house and when you walk by the way and when you lie down and when you rise up" (Deuteronomy 6:6-7). In reference to the law, commands of God, and His acts among the people, the

Israelites are instructed to "make them known to your sons and your grandsons" (4:9).

True discipleship takes place in the home. Parents are to model their faith before their children and they are also to teach them the Word of God. This can be done in many different ways. You can gather the family in an official capacity once a week or more. You can discuss important moral and biblical issues when the family gathers to eat. You can take a moment every morning or night to read the Word and pray. These are just a few ideas of how to get started. The point is to not leave the formation of your child's mind and heart to others. Parents should be personally involved in training up a child in the way he should go, and when he is old he will not depart from it (Proverbs 22:6).

It is my conviction, that parents will give an account to God for how they raised their children. Children are a blessing and an inheritance from the Lord. Parents are to guide and train their children to follow in the footsteps of Jesus, first through their own example, and second through instruction and discipline. A parent who fails to do this will have the blood of their children on their hands if they take a path contrary to God's Word. Father and mother, you are God's watchman in your child's life (Ezekiel 33:1-9). Even though each person has free will and you cannot guarantee what path they will take, you do have the ability, while the child is under your authority, to be an influence for good and a hindrance for evil.

Disciple your family. For what will it profit you to gain others children and lose your own? Yet the legacy of a godly heritage will endure for generations.

Chapter 20
CONFRONTING SIN AND RESOLVING CONFLICT

There is a skill that every believer must develop if he or she is going to grow in Christ and is going to help others grow in their walk with the Lord. That is the ability to confront sin and resolve conflict. It is inevitable when dealing with other broken, imperfect people that there will be disagreements, conflict, and trouble. Yet many people do not know what to do when they run into these situations.

I have noticed that people usually do one of two things when they encounter a problem with someone else. They either ignore the situation or they attack the person directly or indirectly. By ignoring, I mean that they don't address the situation, they hide, or they say everything is okay and create some sort of false peace. They do this at the expense of burying their negative emotions resulting in a poisoned and bitter heart.

When I speak of attacking the person, it can be done directly by actually arguing, cursing, fighting, humiliating, or offending the person. Or indirectly when the offended party gossips, slanders, sabotages, or spreads lies about the other person behind their back.

Both of these paths are unhealthy and unbiblical. I believe there are two passages in particular, that teach a healthy way of confronting someone who has either sinned in their personal life, or sinned against you personally. We need each other and it is never ok to ignore, accept, excuse or condone sin. But there is a healthy way of dealing with these circumstances. This doesn't mean it will always be easy nor that it will always result in a happy ending.

Relationship Over Religion

For some reason people believe that God cares more about our religious rituals, offerings, and worship than how we treat one another. This could not be further from the truth. Somehow as Christians we seem to think that we're okay with God if we serve Him, worship Him, and do many religious activities while our marriage is falling apart, or our homes are in disarray, or there is division and conflict with our brothers and sisters.

In Matthew chapter 5, Jesus comes against this line of thinking. In His great Sermon on the Mount, He starts to debunk traditional and religious thinking that contradicts the heart of God and His Word. He starts off by saying,

> [21] You have heard that the ancients were told, "You shall not commit murder" and "Whoever commits murder shall be liable to the court." [22] But I say to you that everyone who is angry with his brother shall be guilty before the court; and whoever says to his brother, "You good-for-nothing," shall be guilty before the supreme court; and whoever says, "You fool," shall be guilty *enough to go* into the fiery hell. (5:21-22)

In this portion we can see that the people were told and commanded not to murder and that murder would be punished. The command not to murder is found in the Ten

Commandments (Exodus 20:13; Deuteronomy 5:17). And those who broke this command could be judged and receive capital punishment if found guilty (Genesis 9:6; Leviticus 24:17; Exodus 21:12; Numbers 35:30-31).

Yet Jesus wanted to demonstrate that the intent of this command was not just limited to the physical action but that it even included the inner motivation. God's desire was not just to limit physical deaths but even unjustified anger or hatred that led to murder. The anger in this context is a sinful anger, an unnecessary anger, an anger that comes from the flesh, an anger that desires punishment, judgment, and humiliation for the offender instead of being focused on the offense. For that reason, Jesus extends the threat of punishment even towards brothers who are angry with one another.[38]

After saying this He drops the bomb on those of us who think we can still please God with our prayers, sacrifices, and offerings while at the same time our heart isn't right with our brothers. Jesus continues and says, "[23] Therefore if you are presenting your offering at the altar, and there remember that your brother has something against you, [24] leave your offering there before the altar and

---

[38] While this is true, it is important to keep in mind that not all anger is sinful or worthy of punishment. The Bible does say, "BE ANGRY, AND yet DO NOT SIN" (Ephesians 4:26). There are some actions that are worthy of being angry about (i.e. a loved one being murdered, raped, or oppressed). Also, hatred and murder are not the same things, nor are they equally wrong. Nonetheless, they are both sinful. And one (anger) is the spiritual root of the other (murder). And for that reason Jesus is coming against a vindictive spirit, a harbored resentment, a lingering bitterness, and a murderous hatred. As Christians we are called to love our enemies, forgive those who sin against us, bless those who curse us, and pray for those who persecute us.

go; first be reconciled to your brother, and then come and present your offering" (5:23-24). In other words, if your brother has something against you do not proceed to offer anything to God as if everything is okay. Go, fix the situation and then return to do whatever you were doing for God.

Before I proceed any further with this portion, allow me to clarify something from this passage. When this passage says, if you "remember that your brother has something against you" that you should go and be reconciled, it is not referring to someone who is angry or offended with you for any reason. There are some sentimental, easily offended people out there and if you had to stop what you were doing in order to fix the situation every time they were offended with you, you would never get anything done. How often were the religious Pharisees and Sadducees angry with Christ because He confronted their hypocrisy and sin? And sometimes not with very nice terms (see Matthew 23).

If you have to confront sin, injustice, wrong attitudes, or immaturity, people won't always like it. Someone is sure to become offended. So, if you confronted a particular person or group of people with love, respect, wisdom, and according to the Word, then that person or group needs to respond appropriately. This passage is not justifying sin or immaturity in these cases.

Instead, this passage is referring to someone you have actually hurt, sinned against, or offended unjustly. Sometimes this may happen consciously or unconsciously, but either way they have a legitimate grievance against you.

If this is the case, you cannot leave the situation alone, or ignore or overlook what has happened. You need to "first" go and be reconciled to your brother and then you can come back and offer God your worship. You cannot be right with God if you are not right with your brother. God cares more about us having right relationships than superficial religion because we demonstrate our love for Him by the way that we treat our neighbor who is made in His image (1 John 4:20-21).

Jesus ends this portion with these words,

> ²⁵ Make friends quickly with your opponent at law while you are with him on the way, so that your opponent may not hand you over to the judge, and the judge to the officer, and you be thrown into prison. ²⁶ Truly I say to you, you will not come out of there until you have paid up the last cent. (vv25-26)

With these words He is saying that we should fix things quickly with the offended party. Resolving the situation might even include making restitution for the offense. Whatever it costs, Jesus is exhorting us to do it "quickly" before that person goes before God and God passes a judgment that causes us to be disciplined, or in the worst case scenario, punished in a more severe way.

As Far As It Depends On You

Continuing in Matthew chapter 5, Jesus tells us to go and work things out with the person whom we have offended. But what should we do when we are the offended party? Or what should we do if we haven't been sinned against directly, but we are witnesses of something sinful being done by our brother or sister? This is what Jesus has to say.

> ¹⁵ If your brother sins, go and show him his fault in private; if he listens to you, you have won your brother. ¹⁶ But if he does not listen *to you*, take one or two more with you, so that by the mouth of two or three witnesses every fact may be confirmed. ¹⁷ If he refuses to listen to them, tell it to the church; and if he refuses to listen even to the church, let him be to you as a Gentile and a tax collector. ¹⁸ Truly I say to you, whatever you bind on earth shall have been bound in heaven; and whatever you loose on earth shall have been loosed in heaven. (Matthew 18:15-18)

In this passage we are either the witnesses of, or the recipients of someone else's sins. Our brother is the transgressor and we are the offended party. Yet, the first principle we learn from Jesus is that it is our responsibility to go to the person who has sinned, not theirs to come to us. We are to initiate the process of reconciliation. We are not to wait and allow the sin or the offense to grow. Usually this only ends in a growing hostility, bitterness, or hardness of heart.

The second principle is that we should confront this individual in private. If we are trying to reconcile and win the person over, or lead them to repentance, it is very difficult to do that sometimes when it is done in front of others. The person might feel humiliated, or in need to defend themselves in front of a crowd. But when you're able to speak to someone in private it helps to bring their walls down, it helps to demonstrate that your intention is not to humiliate, attack, or condemn them before others.

Talking in private has its advantages. If the person is a coward, liar or a gossiper that likes to say or do things behind people's backs, a face to face encounter will sometimes stop them in their tracks. They will know that they cannot get away with sinning in secret or contaminating others. In these circumstances, the person might be more willing to come clean or stop whatever their doing. However, this whole process should be done with much prayer and love.

This leads to the third principle. The purpose of confronting an individual who sins against us is to win them over. This could be interpreted in multiple ways. In some situations it could mean restoring a broken trust or relationship. In other cases it can mean helping them to realize something they are doing is wrong so that they can repent and turn from their sins. Whatever way you interpret it, you are seeking to correct or restore something that has been violated. We don't confront others just to make ourselves feel better or to intimidate the person. We are seeking to win them over to our side, or God's side.

Now what happens if the person is unwilling to listen to you, or even talk to you? What if you cannot win them over in private? The fourth principle in this passage tells us that we should include others in our effort to win the person over. Paul says in Romans 12:18, "If possible, so far as it depends on you, be at peace with all men." In other words, you should not leave things as they are if your brother won't listen. You need to do everything that is in your power for you both to be at peace or for you to win them over. Once you have done your part, with the right heart and in the right way, you are free from any further obligation. We cannot force, oppress, or violate someone else's free will. Even if they are choosing a negative path.

This step begins with, first, bringing along one or two witnesses, so that "every fact may be confirmed." When a conversation takes place in private it can be your word versus theirs, but once there is more than one person involved, what is said and done can be more easily confirmed and verified. Having more people also means having more perspectives and hopefully additional wisdom. Two or three voices saying the same thing can be more impacting than one. They might even be able to correct or recommend wise advice for both parties involved.

Allow me to give this advice about whoever you choose to bring along into the conversation. First, these should be confidential believers. You do not want any private matters being spread maliciously. Second, these witnesses should be mature believers. By this I mean they are people who know the Word and can counsel according the Bible and not their own opinions. These are people who will actually pray about what's taking place. And also that these are people who have a tested character and a respectable testimony. Lastly, I would advise getting witnesses that will be unbiased and neutral and people that the other person will feel comfortable with. In other words, don't get witnesses that your brother will think are only speaking in your favor because they are close to you or on your side. Remember the purpose is to win your brother over. Neutral voices can be more influential.

Now, if your brother still will not listen then you are to bring the matter to the church. By "the church," Jesus could possibly mean the whole local congregation of believers or even the elders of the church that lead and represent the congregation. If you're not sure which route to take in a particular situation, pray and seek advice from your pastor or leader.

Now, what happens if the person is definitely wrong, and yet they won't repent or listen to anyone? Jesus says, you should have them as a gentile or tax collector. In other words, the church should consider this person a non-believer. They cannot truly be followers of Christ, if they have rejected everyone's love, prayers, and the Word of God.[39] They need to be evangelized. This also means they should be excluded from the membership and fellowship of the Church.

Allow me to elaborate on a very difficult reality at this point. It is Biblical to excommunicate or remove from membership someone who has clearly resisted and stood against Biblical correction by the whole church. How far the consequences should go for any particular sin that a person isn't willing to turn from depends on the leading of

---

[39] This is of course assuming that the issue they are being confronted about is clearly against the Word of God. It's one thing to debate issues that are not clear in Scripture and another to violate something that is clearly taught in the Bible.

the Holy Spirit and the Word of God.

In 1 Corinthians chapter 5, Paul actually tells the church to remove a particular person from their midst (5:2). Paul says he has judged them already (5:3) and that he has "*decided* to deliver such a one to Satan for the destruction of his flesh, so that his spirit may be saved in the day of the Lord Jesus" (5:5). He reasons, "Do you not know that a little leaven leavens the whole lump *of dough?*" (5:6). In other words, uncorrected and unconfronted sin will contaminate and affect the whole church. This of course is not referring to visitors or guests in our churches. Paul says,

> [9] I wrote you in my letter not to associate with immoral people; [10] I *did* not at all *mean* with the immoral people of this world, or with the covetous and swindlers, or with idolaters, for then you would have to go out of the world. [11] But actually, I wrote to you not to associate with any so-called brother if he is an immoral person, or covetous, or an idolater, or a reviler, or a drunkard, or a swindler—not even to eat with such a one. [12] For what have I to do with judging outsiders? Do you not judge those who are within *the church*? [13] But those who are outside, God judges. Remove the wicked man from among yourselves. (5:9-13)

So the decision to remove someone from the membership or fellowship of the church is completely biblical and necessary in certain cases.[40]

That's why Jesus said, "Truly I say to you, whatever you bind on earth shall have been bound in heaven; and whatever you loose on earth shall have been loosed in heaven" (18:18). In this context to "bind" and to "loose" is referring to the decisions or conclusions that the church comes to concerning the particular situation. Whatever they decide on earth will be backed up by heaven if it is based on the Word of God and is being led by the Spirit.

Difficult but Necessary

Confronting sin and resolving conflict isn't always easy. Especially in cases where the matter has to be confronted by the church and ends in someone being removed from the membership. But if the process is done in love, with much prayer, and guided by the Holy Spirit, heaven will back you up even if people don't understand and persecute you. In some cases if a person is cast out, and they are truly interested in serving Christ and being united to His people, they will repent and turn back and the Church should restore such a person in those cases.

If the person never repents then they have only proven the decision was right. John says, "They went out from us, but they were not *really* of us; for if they had been of us, they would have remained with us; but *they went out*, so that it would be shown that they all are not of us" (1 John 2:19). By following through with what the bible

---

[40] See the following passages for supporting verses: Mt. 5:21-26; Mt. 18:15-20; 1 Cor. 5; 2 Cor. 2:5-11; 7:8-12; 2 Thess. 3:6, 14; Rom. 16:17-18; Tit. 3:10-11; 1 Jn. 2:19; 2 Tim. 3:5-7

teaches, you have also delivered the church from being contaminated. Of course it should be our prayers that the person listens to God and repents. And this should never be done with a vengeful spirit.

Beloved reader, I have seen so much in the few years I have been serving Christ. I have seen the consequences of the church not following the Bible in this area. I have seen the devastation, the many lives that are lost (spiritually and physically), and the division it causes in families and the church with my own eyes. I, and many others, have been personally affected through many of these situations and the failure to obey the Word of God. Problems that get swept under the rug do not go away, they just pile up out of sight. Eventually, the cancer that could have been dealt with swiftly spreads throughout the whole body. And instead of one piece being removed, whole body parts are amputated or even the whole person dies.

My heart is saddened and pained with the reality of how many people have been affected negatively because these passages have been neglected. But on the other side, I rejoice when I think of the situations where people have repented, been restored, and churches healed because of its application. If we are going to grow in holiness; if we are to help others grow in their walk with Christ, then we need to be willing to confront sin and resolve conflict.

Chapter 21
WHERE ARE ALL THE BARNABAS'?

Before concluding this book, I would like to speak about someone I believe is sometimes overlooked as one of the greatest examples of a disciple maker. I believe his example will be an encouragement for us to go out and do the same. Ironically, the person I'm speaking about is actually called a "Son of Encouragement." We know him as Barnabas. I believe that as we take a look at his life we will learn some principles on how to be effective disciple makers.

The Life of Barnabas

We first learn about Barnabas in the book of Acts chapter 4. His actual name is Joseph, he was a descendant from the tribe of Levi and born outside of Israel in Cyprus. Yet, we find Barnabas among the apostles in Acts chapter 4 selling his property and laying the money at the apostles feet (4:37). This was a selfless act, an act of great generosity. This is the context in which the apostles nicked named Joseph, Barnabas, "the Son of Encouragement" (4:36). This was a name that, not only reflected his character and personality, as will be seen, but also foreshadowed the type of ministry he would continue to exercise.

The next time Barnabas appears in the book of Acts, he is taking by the hand, an ex-murderer and persecutor of the church, Saul of Tarsus. While everyone else was afraid even to speak with Saul or believe his conversion story, Barnabas was willing to take a chance, embraced him and brought him to the apostles (9:27). He explained and testified concerning the validity of Saul's conversion.

After this, Barnabas shows up again in Acts chapter 11. There were disciples who had been effectively evangelizing and winning souls in a city called Antioch. The church there was growing and the apostles in Jerusalem wanted to send someone there, most likely to confirm that a genuine work of God was taking place and minister to the people. Now, who did they choose for this important task? Yup, you guessed it - Mr. Barnabas.

When he arrived, Luke records, Barnabas "witnessed the grace of God, he rejoiced and began to encourage them all with resolute heart to remain true to the Lord; for he was a good man, and full of the Holy Spirit and of faith. And considerable numbers were brought to the Lord" (11:23-24). Notice, he doesn't arrive like a big shot and starts to criticize and command the church. No, he arrives and begins to encourage them. Another description of his character is then given, and we're told "he was a good man, and full of the Holy Spirit and of faith." In other words, he had pure motives, a pure heart, was helpful, full of power, spiritual; he was positive and fully confident in what the Lord could do.

But to top it off, he demonstrated great humility and wisdom in his next decision. He decided to get the man who had been rejected and sent away by the church in Jerusalem to help him build up the church at Antioch. Acts 11:25-26 says, "and he left for Tarsus to look for Saul; and when he had found him he brought him to Antioch. And for an entire year they met with the church and taught considerable

152

numbers; and the disciples were first called Christians in Antioch."

Barnabas wasn't intimidated nor threatened by Saul. Neither was he seeking to rule and dominate the church at Antioch. Instead, he recognized the talent, grace, potential and ability in Saul and decided to use him. Through the partnership between Barnabas and Saul, a synergy was created that helped expand the kingdom. They became so effective as a church that the city began to call the church "Christians" there for the first time!

From this point forward Barnabas and Saul became a powerful duo and were used in different ways by the church. They were even called to become Church planters, apostles, of the church at Antioch (Acts 13:1-3). They were sent out by the Lord and together they ministered in different cities. It seems that although Barnabas was the more experienced believer he allowed Saul to speak more often (14:12), demonstrating he was able to recognize the grace of God in others and willing to take second place for others to grow.

Yet, the last thing I want to focus on, is not what they both did on their first missionary journey, but what occurred when they were about to go on their second missionary journey.

After some days Paul (Saul's Roman name) said to Barnabas,

> [36] … "Let us return and visit the brethren in every city in which we proclaimed the word of the Lord, and see how they are." [37]

153

Barnabas wanted to take John, called Mark, along with them also. [38] But Paul kept insisting that they should not take him along who had deserted them in Pamphylia and had not gone with them to the work. [39] And there occurred such a sharp disagreement that they separated from one another, and Barnabas took Mark with him and sailed away to Cyprus. [40] But Paul chose Silas and left, being committed by the brethren to the grace of the Lord. (15:36-40)

Paul wanted to make a second trip to strengthen the churches they had already planted plus establish some new ones. When they were deciding who to take along with them, Barnabas brought up Mark's name but Paul was reluctant. How could they trust someone who had previously abandoned them on their first missionary journey?

Although Paul was hesitant to take Mark along, Barnabas wasn't willing to leave him behind. Instead, he was willing to take a risk, give Mark a second chance and invest in his calling. It seems Barnabas' risk paid off. In Colossians 4:10 Paul later names Mark as one of his companions. And at the end of his life, Paul says, "Only Luke is with me. Pick up Mark and bring him with you, for he is useful to me for service" (2 Timothy 4:11).

Barnabas as an example

From beginning to the end, (besides his slip up in Galatians 2), Barnabas demonstrated a very mature and integrate character. He demonstrated what a good disciple maker looks like. From Barnabas we learn disciple makers are:

- Encouragers
- Soul winners
- Willing to invest time and money in others
- Willing to take risks with hard cases
- Bring out the best in others
- Able to see potential in others
- Willing to give second chances to those who fail
- Willing to decrease as others increase and take the lead
- Not jealous of someone else's gifts, talents, and anointing.
- Sold out to Jesus
- Willing to serve and not command or manipulate
- Willing to lead by example

We need more Barnabas'!

Our churches need people who are willing to invest in and encourage those who are new or weak in the faith. It seems that many times we are more concerned with adding numbers to our membership list than seeing those members grow in Christlikeness. My friend, Eddie Huezo says that we need to get rid of the "good luck" ministry in our churches. People will come to Christ, and instead of guiding them by the hand and investing in their growth, we leave them alone and figuratively wish them "good luck" and expect for them to mature on their own. No wonder we have such a poor retention and growth rate in the body of Christ.

How many more Paul's and Mark's would the church see if there were more Barnabas'? How many more churches would get planted, or souls won, or believers mentored, or ministries commenced if there were more Barnabas'? We need more Christians who are willing to stay out of the limelight in order to promote and help build up other people's ministries. We need more Christians to mentor a fatherless and inexperienced generation. We need more encouragers!

But for this to happen time, money, prayers and love has to be invested. Sacrifices have to be made. The Barnabas ministry is needed now. Will you sign up?

CONCLUSION

My desire with this book is that you would be stirred, first, to grow as a disciple yourself. I want us to be more like Christ. The first two sections of this book deal with defining the call, cost, and character of those who would follow Jesus. But the last portion of this book has to do with my second desire. I pray that you would be stirred to connect with other people so that you may, not only help them grow as a Christian, but also create a community where you are able to fulfill the "one another" commands and by doing so grow in Christlikeness.

I urge you, don't be passive about your pursuit of God. Command your soul, stir your spirit, renew your mind, and "seek the Lord while He may be found" (Isaiah 55:6). Do not be conformed to the pattern of this world (Romans 12:2), but set your heart on things above (Colossians 3:2) and "[14] press on toward the goal for the prize of the upward call of God in Christ Jesus. [15] Let us therefore, as many as are perfect, have this attitude; and if in anything you have a different attitude, God will reveal that also to you" (Philippians 3:14-15).

Don't allow failures and setbacks to discourage you from pursuing perfection.[41] All of heaven is in your favor. The Father desires your growth (Jeremiah 29:11). Jesus and the Holy Spirit intercedes on your behalf (Romans 8:26, 34;

---

[41] I would recommend that you read John Wesley's sermon on Christian Perfection, James Arminius dissertation on Romans 7, and Charles G. Finney's lecture on Romans 7. I believe these works do a great job in clearing up misunderstandings of the Christian's struggle against the sin nature and controversial passages like Romans 7. All of these resources are free online.

Hebrews 7:25). You are surrounded by a great cloud of witnesses and have every tool you need to become like Jesus at your disposal (Hebrews 12:1; 2 Peter 1:3).

I believe you can have as much of God as you desire. I believe you can get as close to God as you desire. But what I believe doesn't matter. The question is, do you believe? Then what's stopping you? Go and be Christlike, that is true discipleship.

Appendix A:
DISCIPLES MUST BE DISCIPLINED

I find it necessary to add an additional section to this book that is definitely connected with its theme, though it might not fit in the flow of its chapters. I want to speak about discipline. This word carries so much weight, yet it is able to set people free from normalcy, complacency, and unproductiveness. Discipline is able to set you apart from the common and help you develop into the person God has called you to be.

I will be honest, I am not a disciplined person in many areas. However, I believe it is necessary to be reminded of the importance of such a word.

Defining Discipline

The online Merriam-Webster dictionary has various definitions for the word "discipline." The definitions that best reflect the direction of this chapter are, "control gained by enforcing obedience or order," "self-control," and "training that corrects, molds, or perfects the mental faculties or moral character."[42] I believe the key words in these definitions are "control gained by enforcing," "self-control," and "training that corrects, molds, or perfects."

Discipline has to do with controlling, enforcing, and training one's self with the goal of correcting, perfecting, and gaining. It is in the nature of man to avoid pain and discomfort and instead to seek comfort and pleasure. But a

---

[42] https://www.merriam-webster.com/dictionary/discipline (accessed on 4/20/2019 at 9:21 p.m.)

life of loose living produces poor results, limits potential, and wastes time and resources. Although discipline takes effort and seems restraining, it actually is liberating and creates greater productivity in the life of an individual.

Examples of the Disciplined Life

To most Michael Jordan is known as the greatest N.B.A. player of all time. He has broken numerous records, won multiple championships, and accomplished great feats on the court. Seeing him handling the basketball with such grace, soaring through the air, and moving with great agility truly is a sight to behold.

But how did Jordan become such a legend? Was it because of his superior intellect? Was it because of some physical advantages in his D.N.A.?

Michael Jordan might definitely possess many mental and physical advantages over some, but I believe that he became who he became because of discipline. In various interviews and documentaries he himself would tell you that his success came as a result of discipline, mental and physical; drive, effort, passion, focus, practice, and much training. He could tell you of the thousands of jump shots or hundreds of hours working out and practicing. We have seen the highlights of his abilities, but the real work took place off the screen.

As dedicated as Michael Jordan was to his trade, Paul was even more to his calling. He said things like, "[13] Brethren, I do not regard myself as having laid hold of *it* yet; but one thing *I do*: forgetting what *lies* behind and reaching forward to what *lies* ahead, [14] I press on toward the goal for the prize of the upward call of God in Christ Jesus" (Philippians 3:13-14). "but I discipline my body and make it my slave, so that, after I have preached to others, I myself will not be disqualified" (1 Corinthians 9:27). Paul told Timothy that God has given to us a spirit of "power and love and discipline" (2 Timothy 1:7).

Paul disciplined himself in every way to make sure he accomplished the goals that were set before him. Through his discipline and diligence in spiritual matters, ministry, and character, we now know Paul as one of the greatest Christians who ever lived.

In the same way, we, as disciples of Christ, must be disciplined.

Areas of Cultivating Discipline

There are whole books dedicated to Christian disciplines or areas where Christians need to be diligent, practice and train. But I just want to focus on two: time management and flesh management.

Time management

One of the resources I notice us Christians waste, that we'll never see return to us, is time. Every day, hour, minute, and second that passes can never be gained again. Once it passes it is gone forever. What we did with each moment will be something we will all give account for on the day of judgement.

It is so sad to see how many hours of every day we spend on secular entertainment, worldly pleasures, or ambitious goals. I know of people who will complain that they don't have time to spend with God in prayer, read the Bible, attend church services, serve the community, evangelize the lost or other such godly activities. Yet, they will spend hours playing a video game, or binge watching movies or their favorite T.V. shows. They will spend hours on their phone playing repetitive games, or scrolling through pages on social media. They will spend days, weeks, months, even years pursuing careers, popularity, or money that has nothing to do with what God is calling them to do.

Paul said, "making the most of your time, because the days are evil" (Ephesians 5:16). In other words, take advantage of every minute you have each day and use it in the most productive ways because time is short and things are only going to get worse. Moses prayed that God would "teach us to number our days" (Psalm 90:12). He recognized that we are given a limited amount of time on the earth, possibly 70 or 80 years (v10). And those who do not recognize how quickly those years pass will squander the precious gift of life that God has given to us. But those who take this seriously will live wisely.

How old are you now? How many years do you think you have left? You do know tomorrow isn't promised? When you pass away, what will you have accomplished? What legacy, what inheritance will you leave behind? What mark will you have left on this world or at least on those who knew you? Will you be able to stand before Christ at His tribunal and offer him a pleasing sacrifice?

Richard Baxter (1615-1691), a Puritan

pastor, advised, "Spend your time in nothing which you know must be repented of. Spend it in nothing on which you might not pray for the blessing of God. Spend it in nothing which you could not review with a quiet conscience on your dying bed. Spend it in nothing which you might not safely and properly be found doing if death should surprise you in the act."[43]

Flesh Management

When I speak of the flesh in this portion, I don't mean the sinful nature solely, but also the natural appetites of our body – eating, sleeping, and sex. The corrupting of these God given desires can lead to gluttony, laziness, and immorality. These are themes that many preachers hardly ever touch from the pulpit. They are nonetheless biblical and important to master if we are going to endure in this walk with Christ.

Gluttony is the sin of overeating. Eating fattening or sugary foods is definitely destructive to our health, but it isn't gluttony. A glutton is a person who eats even when he isn't hungry and especially after he is already filled. A glutton is a person that fantasizes with food, eats with his eyes, and his mouth soon follows.

I can tell you that I am overweight and many times have struggled with this area. Eating food is natural and good. But when done in excess falls into sin. I have had

---

[43] Mark. L. Gorveatte, *Lead Like Wesley: Help for Today's Ministry Servants* (Indianapolis, Indiana: Wesleyan Publishing House, 2016), 47.

periods of time of victory in this area but more often than not, failure. Yet that doesn't cause me to ignore the truth that I must gain self-control of this area. In the same way, I want to challenge you to gain control of your eating habits. We should eat to live and not live to eat.

Church history is littered with stories of people who died too young or without seeing the fulfillment of their potential and hard work because they were overweight and didn't care for their body properly.

Laziness is the sin of over-resting and mediocrity. Resting is important and necessary. People who sleep little or work too much have also swung the pendulum in the opposite direction. But resting is so important to God that not only did He rest on the seventh day of creation, He also commanded His people to separate a whole day to rest. Rest helps to rejuvenate and restore strength that has been lost through hard work. Rest helps the mind to become sharp and the body to relax.

Yet, what I have seen in this generation is an exaggeration of this activity. They'll sleep for hours on end. Even if they don't work or go to school, they seem to always be resting, sleeping, and moving about sluggishly. People like this can't be bothered to work hard for themselves, their families, or their churches. If they are forced to work or have some form of responsibility they will do it half-heartedly, imperfectly, and without excellence. A lazy person won't go the extra mile because they'll fall short of going the first.

Here are some things the Bible has to say on

laziness: "For even when we were with you, we used to give you this order: if anyone is not willing to work, then he is not to eat, either" (2 Thessalonians 3:10). "The hand of the diligent will rule, But the slack *hand* will be put to forced labor" (Proverbs 12:24).

> [30] I passed by the field of the sluggard
> And by the vineyard of the
> man lacking sense,
> [31] And behold, it was completely overgrown
> with thistles;
> Its surface was covered with nettles,
> And its stone wall was broken down.
> [32] When I saw, I reflected upon it;
> I looked, *and* received instruction.
> [33] "A little sleep, a little slumber,
> A little folding of the hands to rest,"
> [34] Then your poverty will come *as* a robber
> And your want like an armed man.
> (Proverbs 24:30-34)

The Bible, especially the book of Proverbs, has so much to say on this subject. But I think we get the point. We should work and we should rest. We should sleep what is necessary to stay healthy. Take time off, go on vacations, spend time doing activities of recreation. But discipline yourself to not be lazy. Do everything with excellence and not mediocrely. Time is of the essence.

Lastly, sex was created by God and so was the sexual appetite. But we must be careful not to awaken or feed those desires before time or in a way that is out of the will of God. I have heard from many ministers that our sexual desires are like a stream that God created. As long as the waters stay within the boundaries, it is beautiful and refreshing. But when the waters flood and come out of the God ordained boundaries, it causes damage.

Pornography, masturbation, fornication, adultery, etc., are all sinful corruptions of a godly thing. Stay away from images, conversations, or entertainment that stimulate an ungodly desire or promote an ungodly sexual lifestyle. Women dress modestly. Men renew your minds. "Now flee from youthful lusts and pursue righteousness, faith, love and peace, with those who call on the Lord from a pure heart" (2 Timothy 2:22). "Pay close attention to yourself and to your teaching; persevere in these things, for as you do this you will ensure salvation both for yourself and for those who hear you" (1 Timothy 4:16).

The reason I have brought up these issues of the flesh is because one of my Pastors always used to tell me, "beware of the three G's – Gold, Glory, and Girls"[44] A lack of discipline in these areas have brought down many mighty men.

But a man or a woman who has learned to discipline and crucify her flesh; a man or a woman who has learned to discipline his or her time will become fruitful, productive, powerful and holy Christians. This too is Christlike.

---

[44] You could also alliterate it with F's – "Finances, Fame, and Females."

BIBLIOGRAPHY

Erickson, Millard. *Introducing Christian Doctrine*. Grand Rapids, Michigan: Baker Academic, 2001.

Gorveatte, Mark L. *Lead Like Wesley: Help for Today's Ministry Servants*. Indianapolis, Indiana: Wesleyan Publishing House, 2016.

Liardon, Roberts. *God's Generals: Martyrs*. New Kensington, PA: Whitaker House, 2016.

Lucado, Max. *Just Like Jesus*. Nashville, Tennessee: W Publishing Group, 2003.

McKnight, Scot. *One Life: Jesus Calls, We Follow*. Grand Rapids, MI: Zondervan, 2010.

Merriam Webster Dictionary. "Discipline." Merriam-Webster.com. https://www.merriam-webster.com/dictionary/discipline (accessed 4/20/2019).

Ogden, Greg. *Transforming Discipleship*. Downers Grove, Illinois: Intervarsity Press, 2003.

Wallnau, Lance and Bill Johnson. *Invading Babylon: The 7 Mountain Mandate*. Shippensburg, PA: Destiny Image Publishers, 2013.

Wardle, Terry. *Outrageous Love, Transforming Power*. Siloam Springs, Arkansas: Leafwood Publishers, 2004.

OTHER BOOKS BY THE AUTHOR

Books available on Amazon in both print and kindle form.

If you're seeking to evangelize as Jesus, the apostles, and the early church did, *Christlike: Supernatural* is for you. This book will inspire and empower you to preach the gospel in the power of the Holy Spirit. You will learn how to activate and operate in the spiritual gifts found in the New Testament. They are still for today, and if you are a believer they are for you.

www.ingramcontent.com/pod-product-compliance
Lightning Source LLC
Chambersburg PA
CBHW071531040426
42452CB00008B/978